Tender Bargaining

Also by Carol Cassell

Swept Away: Why Women Fear Their Own Sexuality
Straight from the Heart: How to Talk to
Your Teenager About Love and Sex

Tender Bargaining

NEGOTIATING AN EQUAL PARTNERSHIP
WITH THE MAN YOU LOVE

Carol Cassell, Ph.D.

Lowell House
Los Angeles
Contemporary Books
Chicago

Library of Congress Cataloging-in-Publication Data
Cassell, Carol, 1936–

    Tender Bargaining: Negotiating an Equal Partnership with the Man
You Love / Carol Cassell.

      p.   cm.

    Includes bibliographical references and index.

    ISBN 1-56565-033-6

    1. Marriage.   2. Communication in marriage.   3. Man–woman
relationships.   I. Title.

HQ734.C338   1993

646.7'8—dc20   92-47074

                                   CIP

Requests for such permissions should be addressed to:
Lowell House
2029 Century Park East, Suite 3290
Los Angeles, CA 90067

Publisher: Jack Artenstein
Vice-President/Editor-in-Chief: Janice Gallagher
Director of Publishing Services: Mary D. Aarons
Text design: Carrington Design

Manufactured in the United States of America
10 9 8 7 6 5 4 3 2 1

Contents

Dedication

To the women and men who so generously contributed their personal experiences and wisdom to this book.

Acknowledgments

First and foremost, I thank and acknowledge the many people I interviewed or surveyed who so candidly and graciously provided insight into the dynamics of partnerships.

I owe a special thank you to my editor Janice Gallagher for her uncanny ability to sift the wheat from the chaff, even in the face of much chaff. This book would not have been comtemplated, let alone completed, without her enthusiasm. I am also appreciative for the help and camaraderie of the great team at Lowell House—Peter Hoffman, Bud Sperry, Victoria Hsu, and of course, my publisher Jack Artenstein.

My agent Jonathan Dolger played a major role in making all this happen, and I thank him as well.

A special word of appreciation to Nancy Keith, whose editorial assistance and research made this book come together, page by page, and who worked beyond the call of duty to make this a better book.

To others, who left their mark on these pages, I extend my appreciation—Stella Resnick, Barbara Brown, Marty Klein, Kay Scott, Lydia Neumann, Judy Clymer, Paulette Harrelson, Judy McCallister, Vicki Ramsey, and my brother Philip Miller. I am also indebted to a great many other colleagues and friends for expanding my thinking about men and women's relationships—so many that it's not possible to list each of you, but please know your contributions are very much appreciated. A special thank you to Francis Roe—who influenced this book from start to finish—for suggesting changes with clarity and tact, and sharing his ideas while challenging mine.

My heartfelt gratitude to my wonderful family for their encouragement and support for my work through the best and worst of times, most especially Bob Cassell.

Tender Bargaining

Introduction

LOVE'S GLASS CEILING

We women boldly walk through career doors our mothers feared to knock on, but at home we are up against a baffling, seemingly impenetrable glass ceiling. When we were wed, we looked forward to a real partnership. Now, much to our chagrin, we too often find ourselves stuck in a role we never intended to play: the lesser of two equals, a sort of junior partner.

We all know that the old system, where the woman was the homemaker and the man was the breadwinner, doesn't work anymore. Yet a loving equal partnership, where women and men play interchangeable parts, isn't a reality yet either.

Instead, today's women try to inject equality into an outdated marital structure, and find ourselves fighting the same battles again and again for things we have an equal right to: money, power, time, and—most important of all—a feeling of achievement and parity with our mate.

A woman at one of my seminars lamented, "I thought marriage was about love." Of course it is, and I'm assuming that you love the man you're with. But the unresolved issue of inequality is a source of irritation, like a stone in our shoe, lessening the pleasure of being with the man we love. Both of us would like a traditional homemaking wife to pick up the dry cleaning, fold the laundry, and serve us mashed potatoes and meat loaf when the going gets tough. We women want a mommy-wife, too.

Here is the dilemma. The words we use to describe our deepest desires—marriage, home, children, a life with purpose—may sound the same as those of generations of women before us, but the underlying expectations about our lives differ. Yes, we want a committed relationship, but one that expands our lives, that honors our work. We want a home and a loving man to share it, but we also want equality. Somehow we haven't been able to communicate these feelings to our partners. I constantly hear the same phrase from women across the country: "Men just don't get it." Most men haven't a clue about how to love and live with a woman who takes her own career seriously.

Many women find that he "helps out" but doesn't do his fair share of the grunt work around the house. For others the hot spot is money—even if she brings home a fat paycheck, he keeps the checkbook. Others are frustrated because he expects her to come home from work and cook him a cordon bleu dinner. The demands on our time, attention, and energy makes us feel as if our love life and our career are on a collision course.

Old ways die hard. Men who balk at change are simply responding to the way the roles of husband and wife have been cast for decades. It's a mistake to expect men to give up their traditional manly perks cold turkey. Likewise, it's a dead end for us to stay angry because men drag their feet when it comes to doing a fair share of the household chores. No one relinquishes age-old comforts willingly or easily, husbands and lovers included. That's not the way it should be, but that's the way it is.

When a man agrees to equality with his mate it is generally for practical, not ideological, reasons: he sees it as a way to increase the benefits of an intimate relationship. Once you gain that perspective about why men act the way they do, it frees you to take positive actions and change the status quo.

DON'T GET MAD, GET EQUAL

It took pressure from women to open the doors to medicine, law, and management that had been held tightly shut to them for decades. If you want a more equal partnership with your lover or spouse, you'll have to press for it, just as you have to press for anything else you want.

I empathize with the women who ask, "Why are we always expected to do all of the relationship work?" It's true, women are the designated emotional fire tenders. I wish that weren't so; I would prefer to think that improving relationships isn't women's work but a joint venture between two people who love each other. Don't men desire equality as much as we do? No they don't, and of course it isn't fair. They *should* welcome a stimulating equal partnership on its own merits, but men on the whole are mostly content with the way things are.

Up until now, men have given very little thought to improving their intimate relationships. Why? Because we women do it for them. We demand surprisingly little from men. We tolerate behavior from them we would never accept from a close female friend. But if we are ever to become equal partners with men, we have to start expecting more from them. Above all, *we must become more articulate about what we want our partnership with them to be.*

The good news is that love and equality can, and do, coexist. You don't have to choose between having a good relationship with your mate and having a life that satisfies you. *You can have both. Tender Bargaining* will show you how to attain the kind of custom-built equality you need—you'll design it around your own requirements because you are the one who knows what you want. I'll give you the tools to stop behaving in old, predictable ways and put your energy into creating a new kind of intimacy, one that makes sense for your own dual-career life. You can apply the very same kind of problem-solving techniques you use every day in your professional life to resolve the sources of frustration in your personal life. Tapping in to your workplace competence is the best way to bring about equality in your intimate relationship. In the pages ahead, we'll look at how to transfer your win-win negotiating skills from the office to initiate change at home.

You'll meet women who have been vanguards of change—women who rewrote the script on women's roles. Most are unwitting pioneers; they didn't want a life just like Mom's but they didn't want a career without a man to come home to, either. These women had to create for themselves an equal partnership with their mate, and I hope their experiences will give you fresh insight into how you can do the same.

MY HERO

I can't pretend that the road to an equal partnership is for any one of us easily traveled. But I know it is possible, because like the women in this book, I've done it myself, not in a particularly exemplary way but with much struggle, doubt, and anguish. A few years ago I faced a "roads in the forest" decision: to stay in New York City in a job I loved, or return to Albuquerque to the man I loved. I struggled with the choice for months; it took the need to renew my apartment lease to force my hand. I chose marriage.

Now, even though I work out of a home office when I'm writing, I am determined not to revert to the role of domestic goddess. My husband, Bob, and I not only share the breadwinning load, but everything else: taking out the garbage, the laundry, the checkbook, cooking, cleaning up. It's not a perfect deal. I wish he paid more attention to keeping things tidy, paid bills before they are due, and had more interest in preparing nutritious meals. He wishes, in turn, that I cared less. We argue, and we laugh at our own—and each other's—passionate stances. But we never give up seeking to be two equals, neither one in charge of the other's life or happiness. From time to time, I bemoan the fact that my prince isn't cut from the cloth of heroes, itching to slay dragons for me—but not as much as I used to. At the gut level I know I'm happier marching out in the world shoulder to shoulder with a man rather than being protected, no matter how gilded the cage.

THE JOURNEY AHEAD

Make no mistake, becoming equal partners isn't simply a matter of following up on some hot management tips. There will be some conflict, some arguments—count on it. But these shaky times are not all bad. They improve our relationship because they make us take a good hard look at what is wrong. The reality is that for change to take place in our relationship, we have to be prepared to fasten our seat belts when the road gets bumpy. The key is to look for ways in which love and work pull us together instead of tearing us apart.

1

DO I HAVE TO GIVE UP MY CAREER TO BE LOVED BY YOU?

Wwe are smart, capable women who love our careers, enjoy our independence. Why, then, do we lose our surefooted sense of ourselves in our personal lives? Because we haven't resolved the question of how to divide our energy between the office and the man we love. Somewhere in the back of our heads, we harbor the misgiving that love and career are conflicting priorities. We have an uneasy feeling that our career ambitions cast a long, dark shadow on our love lives. We worry about our careers being sabotaged by romantic distractions. We want to be independent, but we don't want to be alone—nobody in bed, nobody across the breakfast table. Bogged down by conflicting emotions, it's hard to see a way out of the quagmire.

THE TUG OF WAR BETWEEN SUCCESS AND LOVE

Despite the dramatic upscale status women now have in the external world, a residue of subterranean anxieties plagues even the most competent, self-assured woman. Those feelings exist, unacknowledged, unwelcome. At the most unexpected moments they erupt in a burst of lovelorn emotion that is usually triggered by the fear of abandonment and rejection. This stew of anxieties may not simmer in every woman's psyche. For some—Cher, Hillary Clinton, and one Greta Garbo–type woman I met at the airport in Cleveland— these conflicting issues may be resolved. But the rest of us are still a long way from conquering this kind of love-fear mountain.

At the eye of our emotional hurricane is our fear that if we insist on parity, he'll walk away. We know, if not from personal experience, then from the experiences of our friends, that men tend to do a Huck Finn and "light out for the Territory" when the going gets tough, rather than hang in and work out a solution. The killer question: How hard do I dare press him?

The study *American Couples* confirms our worst anxieties. Authors Philip Blumstein and Pepper Schwartz found that men *do* become discontented with their relationship when their mate insists upon a more equitable partnership, and "if a wife's job interferes with what her husband wants from their relationship, he may begin to question the viability of the marriage." Even the men who felt a sense of pride in their wives' work resented being inconvenienced by it. They tended to find her complaints about her job tiresome and upsetting. Or they were so stressed from their own work that they didn't want to be burdened with her problems. The study concluded that when a man feels his mate's career or demands for equity are taking precedence over his needs, he becomes less committed to the relationship.

Faced with the possibility that his discontent will fuel a breakup, a woman's public demands for parity may understandably become muted in the privacy of her home. So much is at risk—love, security, hope. Which is worse: to face being alone again when we enjoy being in a twosome, or to feel undervalued or exploited in our marriage? When our need to be coupled is stronger than our desire for equality, we back down in a domestic "high noon" and crawl back to the status quo if our mate threatens to exit rather than reform. It's an uneven playing field, and we know it.

A woman's need to have a committed man in her life is directly connected to the way we have been taught to be successful. Sociologists label this our "survival socialization." Until the social upheavals of the sixties and seventies, men and women had clear guidelines on what they had to do to survive in this culture. A man achieved security and glory through his work. A woman attached herself to a man and reflected in his glory. A man got demerits if he failed at the workplace. A woman was left without status or resources if she was without a man—doomed to be an object of pity.

It has now been a quarter century since the women's movement began to change those roles, but twenty-five years is not much time in which to assimilate the enormous shifts in personal relationships that equality demands. So we are caught in the crosswinds—abandonment versus autonomy. Our hearts and our minds are out of sync. We want equality with men, but not at the expense of being abandoned by the man we love.

Not surprisingly, then, even women with strong independent goals can be trapped between two sets of ideals, maintains Dr. Willard Gaylin, psychologist and president of Hasting Center, a mental health public policy center. "One set is cognitive, or intellectual, composed of the current expectations and aspirations; but buried within them is a second set of ideals, the residue of what existed before," he explains. In other words, despite the ability of today's women to make their professional marks, we harbor vestiges of the same fear of abandonment that yesterday's women felt when their survival was based on being lovable to a man. Not only have we been taught that we will be loved (and thus successful) if we are charming and feminine, we learned—and this is even more compelling—that we would be *safe*. This belief that we must be loved to be secure in a scary, insecure world is the cause of incredible anguish. We are tugged in two

8

conflicting directions: we long for both our independence and for a man to pull us close under his protective wing when the weather gets stormy. Every self-confident, career-minded woman I know loudly chants the familiar mantra: "I don't need a man to be happy." If only we really believed it.

I remember the day when I was in college, and awarded one of the highest student honors my school could give. At the award ceremony I stood in the glare of the spotlight, weeping uncontrollably. Everyone assumed I was emotionally overcome by the acclaim bestowed upon me by the esteemed faculty and my fellow students. The real story? Of course I was honored, but the tears came straight from my broken heart. The love of my life (Mr. Popularity and Most-Valuable Player on the football team) had taken back his class ring moments before the assembly. How would I react today? Forget him, revel in my moment of glory, one arm raised in triumph, a radiant smile on my face? Or would I be reduced to a soggy mess—a loser at the love game? May I never be put to the test again.

Paradoxically, for all of their love-and-isolation anxieties, some women also fear too much togetherness. "Women have had such a long, distinguished career as caretakers," explains psychologist Erica Abell, "[that] even though they yearn for connectedness, they also fear getting pulled off course, the co-option of their energy by other people's demands." Dr. Ethal Person, director of the Columbia University Center for Psychoanalytic Training and Research, agrees. She sees women postponing marriage because "they fear *loss* of autonomy, and boundaries, becoming swamped—by a man, love, family."

Of course, now that women have gained new muscle in the world, we feel less devastated when we lack a mate. We have friends and our days are full. Yet the grip of our Noah's Ark culture is so strong that if we aren't half of a couple we still feel socially adrift.

Obviously, one of the surest routes to a more equal and satisfying intimate partnership is to conquer our fears of abandonment and rejection. This is a big order. It means we have to resist the notion that our insistence about being equal partners with the man we love will sentence us to a life without a loving man at our side. Before we can even begin to start work on those issues, however, we need to uncover the forces that make us doubt our ability to have both a serious career and a successful personal life.

THE MYTH OF THE FRAZZLED WORKING WOMAN

For years we have been fed a steady diet of bad news about the devastating effect of career ambitions on women's health and happiness. The grim tidings? A working woman is in serious trouble: her health deteriorating, her love life on the edge, she is either going to be left at the altar or find herself divorced.

Sometime in the 1970s a cadre of "stress specialists" burst upon the media scene. Those new darlings of the talk-show circuit solemnly warned women that if we continued "burning the candle at both ends" we would *burn out*. Burnout supposedly caused a wide range of mental and physical illnesses, from dizzy spells to heart attacks. The prophets of doom admonished us that we would wear out before our time, or drop dead from a heart attack, or surely, develop wrinkles beyond even Oil of Olay's healing powers.

Since then, the media mavens have been relentless. Women are tired, depressed. Superwoman is superpooped. She can't get up to full speed at work or at home. Their solutions? Don't work. Be happy. To salvage our health and our marriages, to function on the job—they tell us—we must pare down our aspirations of enjoying *both* a great job and a great man. Settle for less or choose one or the other. As we hear endlessly, the woman who tries to have it all could be left with hardly anything.

Admittedly, it is difficult to believe that so many experts could be so far off the mark about the dire effects of working on the lives of women today. But they are. Dozens of comparative studies on working and unemployed women all point the other way. In fact, a funny thing happened on the way to the collapse of the working woman: it never happened.

Susan Faludi, author of *Backlash: The Undeclared War Against American Women,* compared the health of employed women and nonemployed women. She discovered, "Whether they are professional or blue-collar workers, working women experience less depression than housewives; the more challenging the career, the better their mental and physical health." In terms of stress, sociologists Elaine Wethington of Cornell University and Ronald Kessler of the University of Michigan asked subjects—both men and women—to keep daily "stress diaries." The women reported more stress than the men. *But they also handled it a lot better.*

Having a career even pays off in lower cholesterol levels! Scientists at the University of California at San Diego compared female administrators, managers, and professionals with upper-middle-class homemakers and found that employed women had lower total cholesterol and blood sugar levels, even when life-style factors such as smoking and exercise were adjusted. Their conclusion reflected the obvious: Women who feel in charge of their lives tend to be healthier.

Overall, women who have never been employed have the highest level of depression. They are more susceptible than employed women to mental disorders—from insomnia and nightmares to nervous breakdowns and suicides. Apparently, it's *not* being employed that is a major risk factor for depression in women.

I'm not citing the research about the differences in mental health of working women versus homemakers to set a scenario dividing women into two opposing camps. Rather, it's important to clear the air so women can make informed choices. The information about the effects of working on women's lives has been so off-base and the solution—to go home again or put your career on the back burner—so misguided that the facts can't be ignored.

Certainly, millions of homemakers have satisfying lives, but when we add up all the evidence it's overwhelmingly clear that having a job provides substantial health benefits for women. Even women who are working because they have to—not because they want to—share in these benefits. "Doing it all" may be tough sometimes, but that doesn't negate the very real health benefits of having a job.

Although the media proclaims working mothers to be buckling at the knees from stress, and insists that they yearn to return to the warmth of the kitchen hearth, working mothers themselves don't necessarily agree. Two out of three of the women responding to a survey in *Working Mother* magazine agreed with the statement "Not working would create more strains for me and my children." It's not that moms don't miss their kids at different moments during the day and feel torn between their job and mothering from time to time. Of course they do. And those morning maneuvers, "get out of the house/get to work," and the reverse, "leave work/arrive at home," are a walk on the wild side. But as Faith, a corporate sales representative in Philadelphia and mother of one-year-old Jennifer, expressed it, "I would still work even if my family didn't need the second income. I am learning constantly on the job, and that, I think, makes me a more interesting person." The vast majority of working mothers responding to the survey indicated that working is a plus: 84 percent of these women agreed with the statement "Working makes me feel good about myself, which is good for my children." I'm sure millions of other working moms agree that having a job gives them independence and self-confidence.

Study after study reaffirms that working mothers value being employed. For example, in a study of 442 working mothers, researchers Jeanne Bodin and Bonnie Mitelman found that 90 percent of the respondents prepare the meals, 93 percent handle the marketing and shopping, and 78 percent do the laundry. Even though they weren't thrilled about working a so-called second shift at home after a full shift at work, only 12 percent said they would prefer to give up their jobs and be full-time homemakers and mothers. The working mother likes being employed even when she has a lot to juggle.

I'm not setting out to paint an unrealistically jolly picture of women and work. Women who are out in the work force competing for jobs and for better money and tending to family responsibilities are under a lot of pressure. Still, quitting our jobs and returning to the home front doesn't automatically banish stress. Sociologists from the Wellesley College Center for Research on Women found that women who go from being full-time employees to full-time homemakers report increased symptoms of distress, such as depression and anxiety attacks. The longer a woman works and the more committed she is to the job, the greater her risk of psychological distress when she quits.

What about working part-time, that oft-touted solution for the woman juggling the career, the husband, the kids, the everything? That idea doesn't wash either. The Wellesley researchers found that women who work twenty hours a week or less enjoy fewer mental-health benefits from work because they operate under the fiction that they are only taking on half the responsibility for holding down a job and most part-timers wind up more stressed out than women working full-time.

There are women who *do* feel like a piece of taffy: pulled this way by their job, pulled in the opposite direction by their family. Any woman who is sagging under a bad case of role overload without help in sight might need to cut down on her working hours or arrange for a more flexible working day. Before she takes any action, though, she needs to assess the reality that quitting her job or cutting back won't magically make tension and strife in her personal life disappear. It's easy for a woman to imagine that if she were home digging in the garden, her problems would vanish. Yet the research is clear that stress is not automatically related to the number of roles a person takes on. This means that whatever a woman decides about work, she needs to be cautious about jumping from the fast track to the so-called mommy track before taking a good look at her options.

"There are two ways to look at women and work," says psychologist Rosalind C. Barnett. "One way supposes that you have a limited amount of energy. Each role drains part of that energy, so the more you do, the worse off you are. But the other way, which our work supports, is that having more roles offers women more opportunities to be challenged, to feel competent, and to have their work acknowledged. It also gives them more options, like having more money to hire help to lessen the burden of housework."

Another reward for doing more than one thing is that when something is going poorly in one area, things are likely to be going better in another. Filling more than one role allows us to divide our emotional eggs among several baskets. "The more roles women have, the better off they are, the less likely they are to be depressed or discouraged about their lives," reports psychologist Virginia O'Leary, Ph.D., a visiting scholar at Radcliffe College.

Echoing the same conclusions, demographer Lois Verbrugge of the University of Michigan, who analyzed health data on thousands of women balancing career, marriage, and motherhood roles, found that *not* being involved in meaningful roles leads to depression and boredom.

Most working women can't imagine *not* working. What we do to earn a living is an integral part of our lives. Take, for instance, Brenda, a woman I met in Nashville. She is married, has two young children (one eight years old and one eleven), and holds down a full-time job as a supervisor of sixty-five public health nurses. A full plate indeed. I asked her how her career fits into her life and she responded, "I would never not have a job. I enjoy the challenge, the people I work with, and my paycheck. My family is very important to me, but so is my work. I recently organized flu shots for the elderly at the senior centers in three small rural communities—it was a wonderful experience. I had a ball meeting these people, eating lunch with them, and feeling as though I was really 'doing good.'"

Like Brenda, we relish the hustle and bustle of our lives. What has been fingered as driving women crazy is, in fact, keeping us sane. Betty Friedan, in a *Working Woman* article entitled "Where Do We Go From Here?" gets to the nitty-gritty of the plusses of being employed: "Don't let anybody kid you that for more than a blessed week of peace you would thrive trying to stay at home again. . . . You'd be a fool if you gave up your career for very long, gave up your ability to earn and the control over your life that you simply can't get by being a full-time housewife. It is better in every way for women to have that control over their own lives—better for women's mental health, physical health, happiness, well-being, and sense of self."

THE MAP WITHIN

We know we love the sense of purpose and belonging, the money, the independence we get through our work, and the heady sense that we are in control of our own lives. So why don't we disdainfully spurn the media blitz, reply to it, or at least just get a good laugh from it? In other situations, say at the office, it would be unusual for us *not* to challenge statistical information that doesn't mesh with our own good sense. So what makes us so gullible, so vulnerable to feeling unsure of ourselves in this situation?

The answer is simply that it is hard to get your head out of the water when you are engulfed by a tidal wave of misinformation. The misguided theory that "working exacts several pounds of a woman's soul" is still doled out to us in women's magazines, news features, advice books, and countless television specials.

Maybe the inaccurate, if not bizarre, media stories about the lives of feminist-minded career women can be attributed to the media's notoriously short attention span. Or maybe it can be traced to a backlash—society's attempts to thwart women's demands for equity. As Susan Faludi notes, "Whether delivered in fiery broadsides from the pulpits of televangelists or in discreet sound bites from the drafting boards of Madison Avenue, the message of the backlash remained the same: women who seek true equity will sacrifice true happiness. Feminism, women heard time and again, has proved their worst enemy, stripping them of love, marriage, and motherhood, and yielding only poverty, depression, and drab wardrobes."

Whatever the cause, the effect is the same: the anticareer-women communiqué seeps into our minds, prompting us to feel uncertain about how much of our energy we should devote to work before it nibbles away at our romantic relationship. It distracts us from examining any other cause of stress in our personal lives because we aren't looking in that direction. Worse, it undermines women's self-confidence about how they are living their lives.

"Having it all" has become a pejorative phrase. It's a verbal slap on the wrist for women who aspire to a full, happy life, as if women were greedy and selfish, asking for too much, trying to get too much. As a result, even though we love our jobs, we are prone to attacks of self-doubt when things run amok at home—the car won't start, the chicken is in the freezer and our dinner guests are due shortly, our last pair of panty hose springs a run just as we are dashing out the door. Our work ambitions become an easy target for blame. "Working women tell themselves that if only they didn't work, if only they just tended their family twenty-four hours a day, they would never get stressed out, their children would never get sick, and everyone would always be happy," observes Jo Ann Larsen, a therapist in private practice in Salt Lake City.

We begin to expect the worst, and that expectation has a way of becoming a self-fulfilling prophecy. For example, more than 75 percent of the women in advertising and related fields agreed strongly that a woman can have both a career and a fulfilling family life. Yet one in three confided that she lives in "constant fear that either my career or my home life will unravel." Clearly, women are conflicted and anxious about how to enjoy a complex life that embraces both work and love.

THE NEW FEMALE INADEQUACY

Typically, the media's womanly messages come wrapped in a nostalgic, retro-fifties flag. A prime example is the type of advertisement aimed at the heart and pocketbook of the average career woman:

> My mother was convinced the center of the world was 36 Maplewood Drive. Her idea of a wonderful time was Sunday dinner. She bought UNICEF cards, but what really mattered were the Girl Scouts. . . . I'm beginning to think my mother knew what she was doing.

That pitch, from the October 1990 issue of *Good Housekeeping,* and others like it today are such obvious ploys that it borders on the ridiculous. We see right through it. Right? After all, we would hardly settle for Sunday dinner as the bright spot of our week. But scratch the surface and we aren't so cavalier. Psychologists Rosalind Barnett and Caryl Rivers explain why: "We have never rid ourselves of the fifties propaganda that turned at-home moms into saints and backyard barbecues and station wagons into cultural icons. Many of us still have that outdated postwar map inside our heads."

There has been progress in women's magazines; a few do cover the diverse lives of women today. Still, the display racks in the supermarket are packed with magazines that, either obliquely or overtly, play on working women's ring-around-the-collar kind of guilt. Even more insidious are the increasing numbers of "life-style" magazines and books that urge women to entertain in a lush or unique way—for example, by whipping up a Sunday morning Greek buffet for fifty of your closest friends. The media's latest maneuver is to pressure women to provide "gracious living" for those they love (which, incidentally, requires that they purchase a cornucopia of material goods). Page after page of highly styled magazine photos depicts a life-style that is out of touch for most women, even those earning an impressive salary.

On the other hand, "There is nothing wrong with *Martha Stewart's Living* or with a magazine like *Victoria*," comments author and feminist Betty Friedan, "except that they set standards so high that, willy nilly, they are asking and expecting women to devote themselves to these pursuits, to the exclusion of the richer, fuller, busier life of today's woman."

Although we usually find our way through the confetti of messages floating down on us, when something like the new "lifestyle" standards sticks to us, it makes us susceptible to self-doubt. It's a replay of the old mystique: now it is the Female Inadequacy. Our assurance about combining a career and a home life stalls out when we feel that we don't measure up to either the old *or* the new standard of being a good wife or mom.

"I'm so comfortable at the office and I do so well there that I don't always feel like leaving," says Connie, a personnel director of a corporate health-care company. "I know what's expected of me there. I wish I could say the same for my personal life."

Connie has what she calls a "reasonably good marriage." "But," she adds, "I'm so busy I don't have time to be a big emotional support. Paul knew from day one my work is very important to me. Still, I don't want him to feel as if he is getting the short end of the stick. I try not to work on the weekends so we can spend time together, go out for Sunday brunch, and just hang out. Being married takes a lot more energy than I thought it would. I never feel as if I'm doing right by him or me."

The reason so many women like Connie feel that their career and their love life are on a collision course is that we live in a society that pays only lip service to accepting women's career ambitions. Society hasn't come to terms with the reality that today's typical marriage is a dual-career affair with two sets of job responsibilities, two paychecks, two egos—and a multitude of demands on time, attention, and energy. The workplace is still organized around the way things used to be: men as breadwinners with wives who took care of all the details of running the household, planned their social life, and kept the home fires burning cozily. The unrealistic standard that a working woman can do all the things a full-time homemaker does is a setup for women who feel happy and effective in their jobs to think they are doing something wrong at home. The problem isn't that women are working, it's that neither your spouse nor you has a "wife." But some men haven't noticed.

THE MEN WE LOVE

Educated, liberated, bra-burning women, is how country-western singer K. T. Oslin described women in the eighties and she set forth a challenge, "What are we gonna do about men?" We nineties women are asking ourselves the same thing.

Like many of us, I thought by now we would have made a lot more progress in our relationships with men. I remember vividly a conference I attended years ago in Atlanta. The occasion was an award luncheon honoring Atlanta's then mayor, Andrew Young, who stood at the podium with his acceptance speech. As much as I admire Mr. Young, the sweet smell of dogwood wafting into the hotel meeting room on a perfect spring day in Georgia was making me a little groggy. Then he suddenly shifted gears and put his formal lecture notes aside to talk about what he called the great frontier ahead: "sexual equity in men's and women's personal relationships." He got my attention immediately; I even began taking notes on my table napkin. "You can try to avoid sexism in your public world," he said, "but you can't escape from each other as individuals until you let go of the stereotypes you have of each other. And for men, they face the greatest test—accepting a woman as their equal partner." Andrew Young got a standing ovation. I took my napkin home and pinned it up on the wall of my office, where it still occupies a place of honor.

Despite some bright spots on the equity horizon, many men haven't yet passed that test. Some men continue to struggle with the idea of accepting their mate as their equal. For others, the problem may not be equality between men and women, but rather that having a mate who expects to be treated as an equal partner is a terrible inconvenience. Postfeminist men, for example, say they admire professional women. And I'm sure they do. Yet when it comes down to it, most men don't want to put up with the demands of a two-career household. "I believe in equality but I want a more traditional relationship," is the way Rick, a Boston schoolteacher at one of my seminars, put it. "I want to come home to a dinner, not to a microwave." (The women in the seminar were quick to retort that they want the same thing.)

All good intentions aside, even the most supportive man can get a little cranky or feel neglected if his spouse doesn't take care of him the way his mom took care of his dad. When he arrives home, it may be to an empty house. Or he'll be greeted not with slippers and the evening newspaper but by a partner who is exhausted from *her* long day at the office. Read any of the popular books by men—Robert Bly's *Iron John*, Sam Keen's *Fire in the Belly*, Warren Farrell's *Why Men Are the Way They Are* and *The Myth of Male Power*—and you'll find stories of men bewildered by the shake-up of the old roles and rituals governing how men and women should relate to each other.

For W. W. Meade, a free-lance writer, having a working wife meant change with a capital "C": "When my wife began her career in earnest, it was clear to me how much I was expected to change. No more little dinners, no more laundry service, no more 'Honey, would you call the plumber, carpenter, mason, taxi.' No more careful listening to my troubles. No more king of the hill. What wasn't clear in the beginning was how much change she was working on. It was not the simple matter of dealing with a career. It was a constellation of teaching herself a new way of thinking and being. All I had to learn was how to live with someone who is changing and how not to be mad at someone who no longer pretended that I was the center of the universe."

One of my favorite illustrations of men's bewilderment is an American Express Card advertisement. In it, a thirtyish couple, outfitted in his and hers upscale-casual business suits, is dining out in a swank, candlelit restaurant. The camera catches her in the act of signing the check, her credit card on the table. He looks intently at her (a suspicious expression on his face) and says, "First it was back to school, then a job, now it's an American Express Card. What next?" With an eye-crinkling smile she responds, "You're cute when you're worried."

Cute or not, what makes men really sweat is having to come to grips with the fact that women are earning substantial money. The male-as-breadwinner stereotype is so entrenched that men who identify with that role feel emotionally threatened by wives who are also providers. For example, Ronald C. Kessler and James A. McRae, Jr., social scientists with the University of Michigan's Institute for Social Research, reviewed three decades of research literature and found a downward curve in men's mental health. They concluded, "The increase in distress among men can be attributed, in part, to depression and loss of self-esteem related to the increasing tendency of women to take a job outside of the home." In fact, more men in dual-career marriages suffer psychological stress over the changing

21

profile of the workplace than do men married to homemakers. This is especially true for men who grew up in a world where it was unusual for a wife to work. But it can also be true for other men—of any age—even if they intellectually realize that there is no going back to the traditional marriage.

"Today more and more men are trying to resolve these conflicts in ways that approach the egalitarian," declares Anthony Astrachan in his book *How Men Feel.* "It's seldom easy because the traditional image is so strong. Most men have moments when they feel that they are giving up something that was once important to them, and they wonder if the result is really worth the price. Of course, many men believe it is. A growing minority are thoughtful, cheerful, even enthusiastic about living so their wives' work and their own are equally important. But it's still a struggle and it still can hurt."

The key phrase is, "it's still a struggle." Even the most egalitarian of husbands does not often want to play a secondary role to his wive, either in his own eyes, her eyes, or the eyes of the world. Psychologist Cher Thomas of California State University at Irvine interviewed hundreds of couples and found that in dual-career families men who have working wives are more satisfied with their marriage when their wives act "feminine" at home. "If he has power at work, and she's more traditional at home, it balances off the power edge working wives have," declares Thomas.

The message to women is clear: Although we may stand out in our occupations—lawyer, doctor, or merchant chief—at home we are expected to let hubby take the lead.

Men's resistance to accepting women as equals is at worst a major hurdle to partnership; at the very least it is annoying and frustrating. But there's another, less obvious barrier. We women have to stop being intimidated by the notion that we are being too pushy, too aggressive—that we are expecting too much too soon because we want to have it all.

REFRAMING THE ISSUES

The challenge ahead is to *reframe* the love versus career issues affecting our lives. Reframing the issue means changing the context in which you see a particular set of facts and then taking action based on this fresh insight. Ann Schwanke of the New School for Social Research in New York defines it this way: "Often the actual physical facts of a situation cannot be changed, but by changing the perspective from which we view these facts, we can change the outcome."

Consider how the women's movement reframed our thinking about women's traditional roles. The movers and shakers of the movement—Betty Friedan, Kate Millett, Robin Morgan, Gloria Steinem—helped us see that our problems weren't isolated personal ones, they were political. There was something flawed about society, not about women. And the solution wasn't women adjusting to their roles, it was collective political action to change the roles.

HAVING IT ALL

Our thinking about our place in the world has changed so much that it is difficult to identify with the features in the women's magazines of twenty years ago. Today, motherhood and wifehood are choices, not givens. Now we have to reframe the question of whether or not a working woman can really have it all. This means not allowing society to tell us what makes us happy or what makes us miserable. "Women often take too much responsibility for everything not being perfect," states Albuquerque psychologist Dr. Barbara Brown. "Rather than berating themselves they need to focus on what is positive in their lives. We need to remind ourselves that we aren't omnipotent and stop blaming ourselves for everything that goes wrong or doesn't meet some impossible standard."

When a woman combines roles—professional, wife, mother—what are the real issues at stake for her and her family? It's time to take stock of the costs of juggling roles and obligations, but it's also time to separate truth from fiction. Whether a woman feels stressed or happily busy depends on the combination of roles she takes on and the conditions under which she works and lives—not whether she is employed or not. Women can reframe the question of love versus career by demanding that the dazzling array of options they now have for marriage, motherhood, and careers be fairly rated by society as liberating, not overwhelming.

The most effective way to clear up the myths about the role of work in our lives is to clarify the having-it-all issue on our terms. We don't want to come full circle; we want to draw an entirely new circle. We want home and a loving man, yes, but not without equality, intimacy, and a sharing of household responsibilities. The issue isn't really whether or not a woman can have it all—of course she can. Men certainly have. The issue is that women can't *do* it all. If a man wants a loving partner and home, he has to take on his equal share of the responsibility for maintaining that home. Pure and simple.

No less important is the way women reframe the having-it-all issue for ourselves. We must declare an end to working-woman guilt and embrace a life of work, love, and play. We can reframe the issue by being clear that it is not women who have to adjust to the reality of two wage earners in a family; rather society must put into place support systems for these families.

THE WORKING WIFE VERSUS BEING TAKEN CARE OF

Reframing the old notion that it is a problem for men when a wife is employed means changing the way *we* look at *our* contribution to the partnership. Take, for instance, the way Karen, a top advertising account executive in New York, reframed the issue of her career versus his. When Karen and Douglas were married eight years ago, he earned twice what she earned. Over the last three years her career has skyrocketed; now she earns about what he does. But her advancement is a mixed blessing. She has erratic hours, works late at night, gets up at dawn, and travels all over the country. "The problem began," Karen told me, "when Douglas started to pout, 'Do you *have* to go?' when he saw my suitcase at the door. Worse, he began to withdraw affection. The turning point came when I returned from a trip and he greeted me with a long list of complaints—being stuck watering plants, feeding the cat, picking up the dry cleaning, et cetera, et cetera."

Something about "his whining" made Karen recall a similar situation at her office. "I worked at a small ad agency and handled outside coordination on a major campaign—placating moody clients, playing hardball politics. My partner was the key person on the inside. Every time I returned to the office she bitterly complained that I was never there. One day I got fed up, looked her straight in the eye, and in my best imitation of Bette Davis, spat out, 'You want me to stay in the office? Great. You got it. I'll unpack my suitcase today!' It was the last thing she thought I would say. We both laughed, talked over how to balance the load, and got on with the project.

"I decided I had to do something as radical with Doug to save our marriage. I put my hands on my hips à la Bette and announced, 'If you have a problem with that, I'll just fasten my seat belt, slow down, and take a pay cut. Or I'll quit. What would make you happy?' He was absolutely speechless for a minute. When he regained his composure, he admitted it wasn't what he wanted at all. It was a moment of truth: our life-style would change radically if we had to live on one paycheck, and he liked our life-style.

"The best thing was that it cleared the air. We sat down and talked things over in an honest way without trying to pretend that my promotion wasn't an issue. Life isn't all sweetness and light; I still get exhausted and feel unappreciated, and at times he feels put upon, but it's so much better. The Davis routine, 'Fasten your seat belt,' has become a code phrase each of us uses to put things into perspective when things get edgy. It's worth a laugh and, every time, it brings us closer together."

Granted, Karen's way of approaching the problem may not work for everyone. Hey, we all can't do even a fair imitation of Bette Davis. But when we set the terms of the discussion as Karen did, we move one step closer to uncovering the truth about dual-career relationships: Our partners can't imagine us *not* working.

This doesn't mean that men don't harbor a little wishful thinking about their partner being a woman in a dress-for-success suit with a satin lace teddy underneath it, carrying a briefcase full of homemade chocolate-chip cookies baked just for him. Some research does state that many men are ambivalent toward their wives' career ambitions, but a growing number of studies reveal that a lot of men are not only happy their wives work, but derive great pride and pleasure from their mates' successes. This is particularly the case with highly educated men, such as John, thirty-two, a vice president of a business college. He is a champion for the working wife. "I would have never even considered marrying a woman who wanted to stay home and be taken care of," he claims. "One of the things that attracted me to my wife, Claire, was how dedicated she is to her work."

Witness how Susan, an educational consultant, and her husband, Sam, reframed the issue of work and marriage when she stepped off the homemaker-volunteer bandwagon. Except for a brief career as a kitchen designer, Susan had been a wife and mother. When her daughter went to college, Susan found a unique career niche— leading workshop sessions to enable high-powered private-school board members to resolve conflicts on a variety of issues. "Somehow, without ever talking about it in so many words," she and her husband renegotiated their twenty-year marriage partnership. Susan explains, "Early this week, a call came from a school I've been consulting with in St. Louis. They need to make some immediate decisions, and they asked me to come and lead an urgent session this Saturday for their board of trustees. Doing this means I'll be gone Saturday from daybreak to late evening, and this was supposed to be the first full weekend in months that Sam and I had to ourselves. But he knows that a call saying someone needs my help is, for me, like hearing 'Surf's up!' So he said, 'Go for it,' and I've got my tickets."

Typically, the men I interview say they prefer a woman who can carry her own weight financially, a woman who is successful in her own right. "The last thing I want is someone who doesn't have a strong sense of herself," says Robert Sellers, an assistant professor of psychology at the University of Virginia. "I don't want someone to be Mrs. Robert Sellers. She should have a sense of purpose that is connected to what she may be doing, no matter what that is."

Like Sellers, many men, especially those of the baby boom generation, don't see themselves being married to a stay-at-home wife. Roderick, a lawyer, speaks for a lot of men when he says, "There is nothing glamorous to me about having a wife who doesn't work. I mean, what would you say to her?" Given the proven numbers of men who prefer to have a partner who is employed and enthusiastic about her job, isn't it time for the media to stop pouring out stories about how men suffer if they aren't the primary breadwinners? It's clearly time for all men who prefer equal partnership to say so, loudly and publicly.

THE POWER OF OUR PAYCHECKS

Eventually, the stumbling block of men's acceptance and support for women's career ambitions will diminish. In the meantime, we are wise to concentrate on another major obstacle that keeps us stuck in the role of junior partner in our romantic partnerships: ourselves. Yes, look in the mirror and you will see the Nicest Girl in the Land's reflection.

In my interviews, many a woman sweetly and sincerely insisted that her mate "puts up with a lot" because she is out in the work force. Women—even professionally employed women—will without hesitation award their spouse a gold star for being gracious about supporting their career ambitions. Sometimes they voice the sentiment that they are "lucky" to have such an understanding mate. I haven't heard many women express the belief that their spouse is a hero because he "lets her" have a job, but a few have said just that.

The lingering expectation that a man should be the *real* bread-winner sticks to us like a burr from a cactus, painfully distracting us from the truth: men enjoy enormous benefits from their partners' being employed.

Even among the upscale couples I interviewed, who wouldn't settle for anything less than a dual-career relationship, the game of charades gets played. They act out the fiction that her income is not essential—it is welcomed, wanted, expected—but not essential. Most women do not use the money they earn and contribute to their household as leverage in negotiating for a more equal partnership. Yet in addition to those women who earn between 30 to 40 percent of the couple's income, a substantial percentage of working women bring in over *50 percent* of the combined earnings. True, most women still earn less than their partner, but they do bring home a sizable proportion of the household paychecks. Still, women dogged-ly ignore their power as wage earners. As a result, they don't use that power as an invaluable bargaining chip toward equal partnership.

When I bring up that point in my seminars, and then go on to add that women have to take credit for earning money—money that is necessary for the couple to have the life-style they have or aspire to—I hear a soft swishing sound of eyelashes in motion as women blink. Predictably, this is followed by a wave of nervous giggles. It is as if "we girls" shouldn't be thinking such daring thoughts. It's a terrible dilemma for us. We do love earning money and we take pride in our careers, yet we are very reluctant to call attention to our contribution to the family larder because we don't want to shatter our mate's manly ego.

To reframe this quality-of-life issue when a women works, take a good hard look at how the man in your life benefits enormously from your being employed:

He has more freedom to make changes in his career and pursue more opportunities or dreams than a man who is the sole breadwinner. He doesn't have to stay stuck in a job that he hates, because he has your paycheck as a safety net.

He has the opportunity to be a bigger part of his children's lives than men have had for generations. For example, the "new father"—the man who is an active parent, spending more time with his children—is a direct result of mother's being in the work force. What started out as men baby-sitting for their kids has now blossomed into a new bonding between fathers and their families.

With the uncertainties of the economy, your working provides him a cushion of security. If he is laid off or fired, your paycheck is his insurance policy against being broke. He isn't likely to have to join the ranks of the homeless.

His standard of living is higher because of your income. Even if he earns more than you, your income makes a difference in the comforts of his life. Could he afford everything you have together on his income alone? Could he afford the same mortgage? If you quit work, wouldn't he have to down-grade his life-style?

29

This is not an exhaustive list; I just want to encourage you to think about how your job contributes to making your mate's life more comfortable and less pressured. Instead of asking your partner to share the burdens of a dual-career relationship, you need to reframe the issue. You have to be clear that the money you earn benefits not just you alone, but both of you.

So, no more apologies for our career ambitions!

A UNION OF WORK AND HOME

For too long, women have been warned that in order to have a fulfilling personal life they must leave their work attitudes, values, and behaviors (too masculine, too aggressive) at the threshold of their love cottage. For a romantic relationship to click, we've been told, we should rely on our "feminine" nature—nurturing and championing our spouses.

We can reframe that particular issue by envisioning our at-work persona and our at-home persona as nonopposing aspects of our personality. All of us present different aspects of ourselves to the world, depending on the circumstances. Think about it. According to Adele Scheele, a New York–based career strategist, "We speak to our parents differently than we do our children, or our staff, or our bosses. We might bravely intervene in public to prevent a social disaster but be gripped with anxiety over the need to confront a colleague. Similarly, we might have no problem making smooth business presentations but feel overwhelmed at the prospect of throwing a dinner party for the boss." We can be nurturing and warm and sensitive and hard and incisive—at home or at the office—depending upon the situation. We really are a collection of selves.

We rely on our management skills to smooth over the rough spots at work, and we can use those same insights into human behavior to make things go smoother at home. And vice versa. So don't leave your speaking and listening skills behind at the office. "At home, do the same thing you do at work," advises Paula Ancona, the *Albuquerque Tribune*'s "Working Smarter" columnist: "Speak clearly, without hidden meaning; give lots of positive, specific feedback; involve others when solving problems or making decisions." Ancona offers other effective survival strategies:

> Resist the temptation to be a "jerk" at home after a long day at work. It's easy to let all your positive, cheery traits shine at work and release your crabby, unreasonable qualities at home. But if you expect cooperation, understanding, respect, support, and encouragement from your mate, you'll have to give him the same.

> Schedule at-home appointments or activities on your calendar just as you do work commitments. And treat your partner as if he were an important client. If you're always putting your work priorities ahead of your mate, he can rightly assume that your job comes first.

> Make returning home pleasant for yourself and your spouse. Allow yourself and your spouse at least a few quiet moments to relax and regroup without being responsible for dinner, straightening up, or hearing complaints. Agree not to take it personally when your spouse cashes in on that provision.

In other words, treating our mate as carefully and as strategically as a boss or important client is simply management by common sense. But, you may protest, it's contrived to use management techniques on my lover. Think of it this way: if using our intellect and hard-won job skills results in a more successful love relationship, isn't it worth the mental readjustment? After all, at one time management techniques felt awkward to women in the workplace. Not surprisingly, they rose to the occasion.

Good communication, reaching decisions that please us and others close to us, are just as important—in our intimate relationships as they are in our professional lives—if not more so. Using our work experience to smooth over the potholes in our personal lives just takes practice. Barbara Berg, author of *The Crisis of the Working Mother,* discovered this firsthand. Through trial and error, Berg developed a new approach to managing her personal life while researching her book. Actually, in the last dozen or so years she has more than "managed." She is a whirlwind: earned her doctorate in history, wrote four books, taught classes in medicine and literature at a New York medical school, gave birth to one child, adopted another, and became stepmother to a third. Yet she radiates order and calm and health. Berg is the first to admit that it isn't always easy. Nevertheless, she explains, "I can't imagine my life without my children and I can't imagine my life without my work. The fact that the needs of each don't always mesh perfectly is real, human. I wouldn't have it any other way."

She had to learn to set priorities for her personal life just as she did for her work. One crucial task was setting time limits on projects so they didn't overwhelm her. "You have to choose carefully what you're willing to lose sleep over and forget the old notion of juggling," she says. "Instead, learn to see all your roles as part of a whole. Those juggling acts we all do just don't work; we have to see ourselves as a continuum. If we strive for fluidity rather than fragmentation, women will become complete entities. I think we can have it all, but maybe not always at the same time."

She set a new agenda by abandoning her superwoman act and implementing at home the same technique of delegation she uses at the university to handle a large teaching load. "For me, the asking was hard because for so long I was convinced I *should* be able to handle everything." Eventually, each member of her family took on specific chores; they have family conferences and rely on lists posted on a bulletin board. By using the strategy of setting goals and deadlines to meet them—both at home and at the office—she found the time to pursue her writing in earnest.

Peggy, a sales account representative, discovered how to transfer the assertiveness skills she uses at work to have a more equal partnership at home. She talks about the time she was in training on her job. "I was drumming up business over the phone. My boss listened in on every call and criticized my technique. The more she corrected me, the more flustered I got. After a week of this, I asked for the chance to go it alone, to learn for myself what worked and what didn't. I knew I had the capability to be a top sales producer. I developed my own sales pitch and brought in lots of new customers. I developed a long-range inventory plan and worked out a better system of commission; using my own style made me more successful and happier."

Later, it occurred to Peggy to use her office style to resolve the conflicts she and her husband had over money. "I was hopeless with numbers, so my husband handled our finances. Each month he'd accuse me of overspending. So I challenged him to let me take over the books.

"What an eye-opener! I realized I had been wasting money, but I also came up with creative ways to save—set limits on gift giving, buy kids' clothes in thrift shops, drive to family campgrounds instead of flying to a resort. Our finances improved along with my self-esteem. For once, I felt like my husband's business partner instead of his underling."

There is a good lesson to be learned from women such as Barbara and Peggy: We have to take responsibility for what happens to us.

If we aren't happy with our partnership, we have to ask ourselves what is making us unhappy. What do we want? More decision-making power? Less housework? Time for our own work? Time for ourselves? More cuddling? More say on how money is spent? More support when things go haywire at the office?

Don't hold back. Be honest with yourself about exactly what it is that you desire in your relationship. What do you want to give? What are you willing or unwilling to contribute to the relationship? Are you prepared to leave the paperwork at the office and give your spouse some extra TLC? To do more of the bill paying? Not to watch so much TV? To be more receptive to entertaining? To pick up after yourself?

Taking an inventory includes assessing your partner's attitude. "If your attempts to negotiate a more equal relationship with him are met with a tirade, silence, anger, or any variety of responses that indicate he is unwilling to discuss these matters with you, you need to take a serious look at your situation," advises Francis Roe, physician and author of *Dangerous Practices*. "What he is telling you is, 'No, you are not my equal and I don't feel obligated to discuss these things as if you were.'" His point is well-taken. Still, I firmly believe that most men are potentially willing partners—they're simply unaware of your commitment to creating a more equitable partnership, or are unsure of what to do differently. But if your mate is truly reluctant to talk it out, you'll need to be very clear with him that his attitude puts your relationship at risk.

Taking an honest inventory about what you really want and are willing to give to have a better relationship is more than an interesting exercise, it is your roadmap to an equal partnership. The inventory is a rational approach that enables you to overcome one of the biggest hurdles in achieving a satisfying relationship: the belief that love will always find a way. It might, but we may not like where it takes us.

In his book, *Fire in the Belly*, Sam Keen relates a story about befriending a wise old sage who tells him to ask himself two questions: "Where am I going?" and "Who will go with me?" The sage pauses, then adds, "If you ever get these questions in the wrong order you are in trouble."

We are the first generation of women in history with the opportunity to carve out full-fledged careers and have loving mates and families as well. We women can enjoy the same kind of complex lives men have always had—love, career, family, friends, community work, travel—whatever we like. To make the most of these unprecedented opportunities, it's time to claim a better brand of equal partnership with the man we love. Where am I going, and who am I going with?

2

THE PARTNERSHIP

Passion gets people into bed with
each other; partnership is what keeps
us together over the long run.
                                  —Michael Korda

A s grand as love is, it isn't a magic wand we can wave
over our mate and have our wish for parity come true.
A partnership requires more than words of love and
commitment between two people; it means treating each other
as equals. Most of us—even as we loudly proclaim our commitment to parity—have to admit that relating to each other as
equals day by day is easier said than done. For starters, the rules
about how to live as equal partners don't come readymade. In
the office, the rules of partnership have been long established.
Not so in our personal dual-wage relationships. The up side is
that we are free to try out new ways to make things work for
us. We don't have to abide by yesterday's expectations about
men's and women's roles; we can choose the part we want to
play and write a whole new script.

The down side is that we have to make up that script by
ourselves. There are moments when we can feel as if we are out

there all alone without a flight plan to guide us through the bumpy air of uncharted territory. Dr. David Hopkinson, a Houston clinical psychologist who has developed a specialty in working with partners, advises us to look to the world of business for our inspiration. "Partnerships tend to be alike, no matter what their composition," asserts Hopkinson. "Business partners get tied up in the same emotional knots as do married couples. Both kinds of partnerships even have honeymoons, during which the partners are extra attentive and flexible, followed by a period of sorting out and maturing. Business expansion and the birth of children engender similar stress for the respective partnerships."

Hopkinson's theory that business partnerships are like marriages, and vice versa, points us in the right direction. In many ways, intimate partners *are* in business together—real estate, automobile maintenance, purchasing goods and services. Thinking of our love relationship in this light helps us see that to build a better model of equal partnership, we can bring home something we use every day at the office: our ability to work with people. We have a wealth of management and decision-making experiences we can apply to situations in our personal lives. Be aware, however, that this suggestion comes with a warning label. Our intimate partnership is *love centered*—we are a merger of lovers, not a merger of business interests. We love our partner, so we have a keener interest in every nuance of that relationship; we envision being together in our golden years. Our business relationships may have a future, but the emotional connection to our business partners leans toward the legal agreements and joint ventures of the relationship.

In our intimate partnership, if the love withers, an agreement to wash the dog or go to your parents' home for the holidays isn't worth much. We don't have the recourse of a personnel department where we can file a grievance against our spouse. The challenge is how to have a partnership that rationally divides both the benefits and the obligations of a relationship without losing a sense of the heady, irrational passion that brings us together. A man and a woman attempting to excel in their own careers while trying to merge into being a loving couple who share responsibilities and decision making are dancing a complex *pas de deux.*

This means practicing a lot of fancy footwork to make our brave new lovers-as-equals partnership work. "There's got to be an awful lot of dialogue because the rules are new. Each of us has got to pull some weight and make some compromises," advises Johnnetta Cole, who balances the demands of family against her duties as president of Atlanta's Spellman College. Before we learn how to do that, let's define our terms.

Obviously, the definition of an equal partnership depends upon the individuals involved, their situation, and other factors. Still, there are some common themes.

Psychologist Sol Gordon describes an egalitarian relationship this way: "[It] does not demand that the man automatically forgo the role of breadwinner, nor does it dictate that a woman can't cook and prepare all the meals if this arrangement is based upon mutual agreement. What an egalitarian relationship does demand is a commitment to equal opportunities in decision making, specifically including choices related to career, child rearing, and life-style questions." Another insight into the dynamics of an equal partnership is offered by therapists Dr. Sonya Rhodes and Dr. Marlin Potash. "Both partners," they explain, "do the emotional and physical 'chores' of a relationship, sharing their emotional lives and coping openly with issues of power and control, sexual and otherwise."

For a relationship to be successful, the details of the form and shape of the partnership must be worked out with a sense of fairness and respect for each other's wants and needs. Although these details vary, in a relationship of equals neither partner's aspirations or lifestyle is more important than the other's. No one's time is more important than the other's, no one is in charge of the other, and each picks up his or her own "stuff."

Still, despite all the logic we apply to understanding the dynamics of equity, despite all the effort we put into finding exactly the right words to describe the kind of partnership we yearn for, there is another dimension. What counts the most is gazing across the table at the man we love and feeling that all is right with the world because we are in this together.

THE TREMENDOUS TRIFLES

Our changing expectations of ourselves and each other become obvious when we divide up the most mundane tasks. Who *should* do what? Who takes out the trash? Who stays home from the office to wait for the electrician to fix the air conditioner? Who will take the kids to soccer practice?

Dividing up tasks doesn't make it necessary or even desirable for men and women to have identical roles. Rather, equality is in the *spirit* of a relationship: each partner pulls his or her own weight and at the same time they pull together, each contributing in a different way to the partnership. But don't confuse this concept with the old notion that relationships have to be weighed carefully on a perfectly divided scale, half his, half hers. Instead, it helps to envision a partnership as a "balanced relationship," one in which each person gets what he or she wants. If, however, one or the other of you perceives yourself to be giving more than you're getting, or getting more than you're giving, things will get off kilter very quickly.

When they do, conflict can erupt and spread like a brushfire. We get in a tizzy, ready to go to the mat over the slightest show of our partner's irresponsibility: he is five minutes late, he forgot to screw the cap on the ketchup bottle, he left the car's gas tank on empty, he finished the ice cream and put the carton back in the fridge. Who gets to choose what TV show to watch takes on cosmic proportions—as though the world is ending and this is our last chance to see "The Love Connection."

To a bystander, these arguments seem inconsequential. But these battles are not about dust, empty cartons of ice cream, or errands; they are what I call "tremendous trifles." They are the real-life dilemmas that generate profound questions about how we deal with each other and how we want to live our one precious *life*.

To what extent is it right or fair that one person have the giant share of responsibility for earning a living and the other be in charge of the housework, the children, and holiday gift buying and celebrations? How right or fair is it that one person has substantially more leisure time than the other? Should one person be on the fast track while the other is expected to put a career on hold? The struggle for answers is really a battle to determine whose needs—or perceptions of needs—should take precedence.

The dismal truth is that we'll stay stuck in an endless round of debates about "shoulds" until we change our tactics. It's too easy to get emotionally involved trying to protect our turf; we need to step outside our arguments and see them from another perspective. Stop and consider how the delegation of tasks and responsibilities is handled in the workplace. From time to time we might have a discussion with our colleagues or our supervisor about who should do what, but essentially we have a job description, labor agreement, a consultant contract, or personnel handbook to guide us. Even though there may be a lot of give-and-take and discussion about what the job entails, the final draft of the document is signed off by the person who has the most power or the final authority to make that decision.

The final-authority model is the way traditional marriages are structured, the husband being the final authority. Wives in these marriages are not powerless, but their power to make unilateral decisions is limited; the husband makes the final cut. It is easy to analyze the power structure in those situations because most of us grew up in a traditional household. If our mothers were employed (and many were) their jobs tended to be in family businesses or in traditionally female professions such as nursing and teaching. After their first child arrived, these women tended to leave their careers, never to return. In our two-paycheck relationships, the power structure isn't as clear cut because our relationships are in transition—not quite egalitarian, not quite traditional. Putting an end to those "who-should" disputes rests heavily on understanding the issue of power, who has it, and what they do with it.

WOMEN, MEN, AND POWER

Power can be defined in many ways, but for our purposes it is the ability to impose one's will on others, or the ability to alter another person's choice. But power doesn't exist by itself; it is influenced by authority and control. Just because a person is exceptionally gifted with natural leadership qualities doesn't give him or her the authority to lead or rule others. Authority is derived from and based upon social norms and expectations. For example, simply by virtue of holding a certain position, such as boss, teacher, or judge, people automatically acquire the authority to establish rules.

Control, on the other hand, can be explicit or subtle, but is decidedly personal. Essentially, control takes the form of pressuring or appealing to the other person in order to get him to carry out your wishes.

Does the concept that one has to have authority and exert control to get what they want seem cold, manipulative, and selfish to you? Does it offend you? It wouldn't be surprising if you feel that way. As women, we have been taught that women who seek or use power are unfeminine or are the Queen bees. Men, on the other hand, rarely have any trouble with the concept of power. They feel entitled to power and the trappings that go with it, because that's what they have been taught.

For women, power has always had a negative aroma. Maureen Dowd, a *New York Times* reporter, is on target with this observation: "Women were raised to believe that they should get their way indirectly, through cajoling and flattery. They were not taught to say, in the memorable phrase of former White House Chief of Staff John Sununu, 'I'll chain-saw your balls off.'" Unfortunately, our fear of power is not just an appealing spin-off of our femininity. It actually does us harm because it keeps us caught in the same old frustrating patterns.

USING POWER

On the job, women are getting much better about accepting the realities of power and the need to influence colleagues to see or do things our way. Most of us know by now, through our own experience, how to play the office power game of jockeying for position or money or recognition. We have learned that whether we are molding the direction of a team, selling an idea, or maneuvering our way through a budget, we need to exert influence over others to gain their support.

The issue of who has power and the authority to say aye or nay to our desires is obvious when the person you are dealing with is your boss. But when individuals are at the same level—peers or coworkers—getting your own way is more delicate. This is an important point because conceptually, our relationship with our mate is a long-term relationship of peers. According to Linda Hill, an associate professor of business administration at the Harvard Business School, we do well to think of our office peers as long-term allies. "Even if you don't need them right away, you will later," she says. "The key to influencing others is in the amount of credibility and trust built up between the people involved." With the obvious differences that we are lover-peers, developing an egalitarian partnership with our mate means using the same basic strategies built on credibility and trust that we use to get support from our colleagues and peers at the office. It's a reciprocal power arrangement; in order for us to have their support, they must feel that we'll support them when they need it.

Just as power pervades all aspects of the workplace, power also pervades all aspects of our intimate relationship. In fact, if you've never experienced a power struggle, you've never had a close relationship. Power struggles occur between parents and children, siblings, neighbors, friends, and, of course, spouses. The more intense the emotional involvement, the greater the likelihood of struggle. "A classic power struggle involves two people fighting over the same apparently scarce resource," observes clinical psychologist Susan Campbell. "This scarce resource may equate to such intangibles as being right, having things done a certain way, being treated a certain way, and the like. Or the struggle may involve more tangible items such as money, time, space, or fringe benefits."

Whatever it is that we want a fair or bigger share of, the real struggle is not about that share, but about who is in charge. Marie Richmond-Abbott, author of *Masculine and Feminine,* writes that "power is always an underlying factor in a marriage. Its influence may only surface in time of conflict, but both partners are aware of the underlying power positions." Schwartz and Blumstein, the authors of *American Couples,* clearly agreed. They organized their landmark study around the concept of power: who has the resources, who makes the decisions, how conflict develops, and how it is negotiated.

Pinpointing exactly how couples make decisions and which partner wields the most power isn't simple. Take, for instance, a couple we'll call John and Mary, and a shopping expedition. Scene one: Mary wants John to go shopping with her. Scene two: he declines; actually, he refuses to go. Final scene: we find Mary and John at the mall shopping. Since John went shopping even though he initially was reluctant to do so, Mary, at least at face value, has exerted power over him. However, what we don't know is how Mary persuaded John to go to the shopping mall or how reluctant John really was in the first place. Maybe he just needed to be coaxed a little, or maybe it took Mary every bit of control and authority she possesses to get him out the front door. Maybe she somehow bribed him.

Which leads us to the next point. Power is not just an outcome (whose wishes prevailed) but a process (how the decision was reached). Even if we were privy to what methods Mary used to convince John to go shopping, we would have an incomplete picture of who has the most or the least power. Why? Because the balance of power between two people is not a fixed item, but rather is fluid, always in progress. Power can shift from one spouse to the other. And, at any particular time, one spouse may have more power in certain areas of the relationship while the other spouse has more power in others.

Further complicating the picture is that most men and women use power very differently. Traditionally, men exercise a formal, authoritarian style of power, while women are more flexible and democratic. On the job, some women do follow the Godzilla/Donald Trump male model, but most women use a distinctive female modus operandi. According to reporter Maureen Dowd, "Studies and interviews with top executives show that the second wave of women in management do not use the male style of leadership. They are less dependent on formal authority and believe more in the power of personality. They lead by charisma, not fear, sharing power and including others in decision making. And they motivate their staffers by building self-respect, not by intimidation." Dowd goes on to say, "Most successful women describe their power as chameleonlike: changing to fit each person and situation, ranging from steel and ice to sugar and spice." And flexibility is a plus for women. Because we don't want power in order to *prove* something as much as to *accomplish* something, we are flexible about the rituals of one-upmanship. "I don't mind fetching coffee," explains Judy Clymer, the co-owner of a medical supply firm, "as long as I'm getting one for me, too, and I'm sitting at the same table."

Although the pace of change in how women achieve and wield power in the workplace has been maddeningly slow, it has been sure. Now we wrestle with the hard part: getting our fair share of power in our marriages. As Darla, married for twenty years and an engineering clerk for a major communications company, told me, "I would like to feel and act as if my feelings and needs are as important as my husband's. I don't want to be treated like a child and I don't want to take the role of parent to get my husband to help me with the household responsibilities or decisions. I refuse to allow us to repeat the roles of my mother and father—both of whom worked full-time. She worked a lot harder than he did."

Getting a fairer shake in our intimate relationship means transferring from the office to our home our knowledge about achieving power and influencing others. Let's begin by taking a fresh look at what is causing a power struggle between ourselves and our mates. What is it that we do as individuals, and what is it that each of us does as half of a couple to maintain the status quo? Who resists change the most? And why? After we answer these questions, we must accept the reality that insisting upon an equal-partner relationship takes not only a commitment to the cause but a wallop of energy. As we scramble to invent a way to balance our responsibilities more equitably, remember that we are pitted against a long history of social norms dictating who should work outside the house (men), and who inside (women).

The experiences of Elizabeth, owner of a training and assessment firm, illustrate the point. When Elizabeth married eight years ago, she was an executive secretary in an educational consulting firm. Five years later, she felt it was time to apply what she had learned about educational evaluation methods to start her own business. She found that, just as women are creating new roles for themselves in the workplace, they can overhaul their at-home roles. "I feel to a large degree, I create my role," she wrote me. "Obviously, there are influences on me: my parents, his parents, what the culture says. These forces are difficult to evaluate and sometimes to overcome. For example, the division of labor carries wider connotations and we've had to do so much discussion to arrive at a comfortable level and division. And I still cook—but I have become good at it and he does the cleanup and dishes. Did *that* involve a lot of adjustment! But I don't think you should let those issues slide. I've seen too many woman martyrs and I have no intention of being one."

Don't we all echo Elizabeth's sentiment? We have no intention of wearing the mantle of martyrdom. At the same time, we get tripped up by our lack of experience with equal partnership.

THE SYSTEMS APPROACH

An egalitarian partnership is a lot harder to achieve and maintain than the traditional employee/boss relationship. A two-person partnership makes for a poor decision-making machine. When two people don't agree on an issue, every vote will end up in a tie. That's why astronaut teams are usually composed of odd numbers, as is the Supreme Court. How, then, do partners in a dyad make a decision? According to Houston business writer Teresa Byrne-Dodge, decision making usually breaks down into two camps. One is a consensus model involving long discussions. "It builds a sense of equality and worth on the part of both partners, but it is notoriously inefficient, frustrating, and slow." The other model is the executive model, in which one partner insists upon getting his or her way or uses authority or control to get his or her way. "It is efficient and rapid, but smothers dissent, breeds morale problems, and in the long run can be destructive to the partnership."

But there is another way to go about making decisions. We don't need to choose either a consensus or an executive approach to resolve our differences. We can put to rest those old moral-high-ground arguments about who "should" do what, when, and how. The most effective way to deal with decision making is to work out a system—a system that not only specifies who is responsible for decision making, but also who is responsible for carrying decisions out. For example, if the couple wants a car, someone must decide when to buy it, what make and model to buy, and how to finance the purchase. Then, someone has to carry out these decisions by shopping for it and arranging for the loan.

The first step toward working out a system for making decisions is to consider the dynamics of your relationship and look at how decision-making power is divided up between you and your mate.

In a *shared-power relationship,* the couple jointly makes all major decisions and discusses each situation as it arises. In a *separate-power relationship,* the couple divides the areas of power and each is primarily responsible for the decisions in his or her area. In a *joint-power structure,* each partner assumes responsibility for some areas, but the couple makes joint decisions in others. Each takes the leading role in the areas in which he or she has the most expertise. Often, the decision falls to the one who is most involved or passionate about a particular choice. When neither has more expertise or interest than the other, they make the decision together.

There really are no clear boundaries from one style to the other. Most couples tend to use one style in one situation and another when a different situation merits it. Whatever style we adopt, we don't want to overlook the fact that our emotional needs—all the intimate, delicate facets of a personal relationship—are as much a part of the process of living with another person as working out the family budget or assigning household chores, and a whole lot more important.

THE THREE POWER OPTIONS: SHARED, SEPARATE, AND JOINT

Let's begin with a look at how the three basic types of systems are expressed in the day-to-day business of being a couple. Note particularly how these couples revamped their decision-making structure to match the changes that came about in their lives.

Over twenty years of marriage, Shirley, the owner of a graphic design business, has through trial and error (mostly trial, she says) reached different agreements with her husband, Jack, about how they will manage a two-career life. Shirley describes their current style as mostly a shared-power agreement. "At first," remembers Shirley, "we did everything together—laundry, bill paying, everything. It was the early seventies; we were both sociology students, and we were determined not to have a conventional arrangement of his-and-her roles. We were not only cool, we both were card-carrying feminists. Our money, our vacations, who watched what television show, no matter what the decision was, we just tried to come to a solution in an equitable way." Their equal-share plan fell apart when their twins were born in the early eighties. Shirley quit her job and they "more or less" dissolved into the traditional mommy and daddy roles. "It was okay, but I mostly resented having to do most of the housework," Shirley ruefully recalls. "Three years later we had to shift gears, because I began my own business. We divided up what had to be done and rotated who did what; I did the laundry one week, he did it the next, and so forth. We were very careful to do exactly our fair share and no more.

"At my office, I used more or less the same concept and rotated tasks among my employees. I put great stock in management charts to organize the office. But it's a very small office of three people, and I began to see that it is more efficient for everyone to just pitch in and do whatever has to be done. At home, it took me a while, but I finally realized that we would be a lot happier if we retired the rotating system. Our system is very informal; we don't actually divide up the responsibilities as we used to, and we aren't so obsessed with everything being precisely equal. It's more 'share and share alike,' which suits the way we live now."

Joan's management style led her to develop a separate-power system in her marriage. Joan is, as she puts it, "a list maker. At my office I couldn't function without a list of prioritized things to be done. I make one for each project I'm working on. They help me organize what to tackle when and keep me from wasting time.

"At home, I was less efficient. After I'd been married for a year, I felt I was sinking fast at home because I could never see anything finished. Everything was always in disarray, in some stage or another of being completed. I would put the clothes in the washer but couldn't remember to get them out of the dryer. Ron was willing to do his fair share but wasn't very good at remembering just what that was. One time we had dinner guests and when I walked in the door I discovered he had forgotten to put the roast in the oven. I was furious. A few days later, I brought home a pile of work from the office. Ron was looking over my shoulder as I consulted my list and suggested we use my list approach to divide up our home chores.

"Now, Ron and I make lists constantly and split everything half and half: chores, laundry, bills." Besides the division of household work, Joan tells me that each has the power to make decisions in their own sphere. She explains, "He is in charge of running the household, the shopping, and generally the running-errands stuff. I cook, manage our money, and take responsibility for dealing with maintenance (plumbers, repair people, et cetera) and the social networking. I pick out where we go on vacations because he doesn't want to bother. He takes care of the logistics once we get there because I don't like doing that. There are a lot of things we do discuss and come up with a decision together—from how we will pay the mortgage to who we would like to have over for dinner. It helps that we agree on almost everything, so it's easy to make a decision that we can both live with."

Jan and Alan Wilson's two-job, two-toddler household is on a tight schedule. As a deputy state land commissioner, Jan commutes from Albuquerque to Santa Fe five days a week. Alan works long hours in his Albuquerque law firm. Jan says that neither she nor Alan expected this life-style. They started out with a fairly traditional marriage, but all that changed when Jan joined the land commission staff. Feeling the pressure of a new, very political job, Jan focused her priorities on work. Consequently, Alan had to take a major role in keeping the household together. After a few months, he felt he was unfairly burdened. Jan began to realize that just as she had to negotiate on her job with people having very different priorities and interests—but common goals—she and Alan would have to sit down at the bargaining table to hash out a better system to deal with the changes in their lives. And that system meant splitting up their roles and responsibilities into a joint-power arrangement. They found that taking shifts and sticking to them was the only way to get everything done. Alan now is the Master of the Universe from 7:00 to 9:00 A.M., while Jan wears a Supermom cape from 6:00 to 8:00 P.M. The revised schedule allows Jan to get to her job in Santa Fe on time and gives Alan the flexibility to work a little late. They modify the system when the need arises by remaining willing to rewrite the rules along the way.

Despite some jangled nerves from time to time, they are both quick to say that their marriage has benefitted from the arrangement. "There's a lot of excitement that comes with both of us getting on the career path," enthuses Alan. "It's been great for her and for me."

"BUT YOU PROMISED"

Even the most effective decision-making system won't likely be a forever-and-ever deal. You'll have to amend it as you change, both as individuals and as a couple, or as something changes in your lives—a promotion, a job transfer, a baby.

When your partnership begins to feel frayed around the edges, read it as a signal that your decision-making system may not be working for you anymore. You may need to do something drastic, such as write it off and start from scratch. Or you may simply need to modify what you are already doing.

What holds some people back from rethinking their situation is a blind loyalty to the past. They adhere to the notion that once a system is in place, they are honor bound to stick with it. It's the ghost of "But you promised." Certainly keeping promises is important, but at the risk of sounding blasphemous, a promise is not a sacred vow. A change in our circumstances can make it impossible to fulfill a promise that was sincerely made. For example, let's say that four years ago you promised your mate you would go anywhere he went—a sort of modern-day Ruth. Now he has a job opportunity that could mean relocating and the promise you made has come back to haunt you. Four years ago your career was less promising. Now it has taken off and you are in line for a good promotion. Maybe you aren't facing a career issue but a roots issue. You feel reluctant to pull up roots and move because you have become very attached to your house and neighborhood. Let's take another, less dramatic situation: you took on the responsibility to be the bill payer for a year. Now your travel schedule is making it impossible to fulfill the task—the bills stack up and become overdue.

Making readjustments in a plan is not an irresponsible action or "going back on your word." All successful organizations adapt to changes in their environment. They all have some type of plan for meeting their goals; for some reason, five-year plans are the most common. But a corporation couldn't thrive and endure if its plan were etched in stone. Plans are constantly revised to better deal with changes in the environment, such as a shifting economy, an unexpected opportunity, the incapacity or death of a significant person in the organization, or the appearance of a new kind of technology. Not so long ago, few small businesses had a facsimile machine; now it's rare that one doesn't. Sending a letter across the continent takes a mere push of a button. Hence, prefacsimile budgets had to be adjusted to include this new technology and businesses had to revamp the system they used to handle communications.

It's the same with our intimate partnership's plans. We need to update and revise them from time to time in order to more accurately go along with the ebb and flow of our lives. Think of your decision-making system as a long-range business plan, one with goals and objectives, but one responsive to the changing environment. Don't hold your partner hostage because "he promised" or allow yourself to be trapped by a promise you can't in good conscience keep because it doesn't make sense anymore.

No matter how much we experiment with the shape and form of our relationship, the fundamental tenet of equality is that the couple's roles and responsibilities are mutually agreed upon and freely chosen. If not, it is a faux partnership, and we'll have to go back to the drawing board and work out a system that both partners feel they can live with.

AVOIDING GETTING SIDETRACKED

When you put a new system in place or modify an old one, be aware that some tension is unavoidable. There is always discomfort in adjusting to new rules, and most of us resist implementing changes in the way things are done; it's not easy at the office, and it's not easy at home. We are all creatures of habit, even when the habit isn't satisfying. By anticipating some discord, you can avoid getting sidetracked from initiating a new system that accommodates the needs and goals of both of you. Remember that when things are on an even keel and we are in a state of lovers' bliss, we scramble to take the credit for communicating so well. But when things aren't going well, we tend to pin disappointments and frustrations with our partnership on our partner. Our mate is, unfortunately, a convenient scapegoat. As therapists Connell Cowan and Melvyn Kinder impress upon us, "It is a lot easier to feel sorry for ourselves and to blame someone else for our misery than it is to assume responsibility for our own well-being."

Not only is putting the blame on our partner unjust, it is self-defeating. It reinforces a sense of passivity, makes us feel as if we can't really change anything, and drains our energy away from our partnership. We must direct our energy where it really counts: toward being allies for each other's hopes and dreams.

When things get edgy, it helps to remember that despite an intimate relationship's shortcomings, there is much that tips the scales in its favor. It's cozy and delicious to cuddle in bed with the same man every night, it's sweet to wake up with him every morning. It's reassuring to know that he'll be around if we're promoted or fired, if we get seriously ill, or if we merely come down with the flu. Life is hard, and it's easier when someone loves us and is in it with us for the long haul.

THE GLUE

Working out the details of an equal partnership often means resolving nitty-gritty problems. But you can't allow those negotiations to overshadow the real pleasure of being partners. Don't get lost in the tremendous trifles and lose sight of the big picture—the two of you marching side by side can conquer mountains together.

Author Francis Roe goes directly to the heartbeat of the most successful partnerships: a shared goal. "It's important to share a goal," he explains, "because having a master plan gives a couple a sense of a shared destiny. Knowing you are working together toward something significant puts the little petty things about a relationship into perspective."

Don't confuse this shared-goals concept as a new twist on, or a throwback to, the fifties "togetherness" ideal that smothered so many women's options. It's important to recognize the difference, because many women worry that any pluses we gain from teaming up with our partner results in a loss of individuality. This fear is understandable. We have struggled long and hard to erase the traditional teaching that there is no higher plane of womanhood than sacrifice of self on the altar of togetherness. No wonder we are suspicious of any proposal to share goals. It feels like a step backward. So let's reframe the issue: sharing a grand design doesn't mean that either partner must give up or dilute his or her life ambitions to achieve something for the benefit of the partnership. Rather, in addition to pursuing our individual objectives, we can harness the energy created by our being together.

The partnership of Katherine and Gary gives us a wonderful example of this sort of synergy. Married for three years, she is an editor with a university press and he is a professor of English. Working together on a common goal wasn't in their plan when they married; each had a full agenda to deal with separately. Now, they are enthusiastic about a joint venture. As Gary tells me, "One Sunday we were sitting around reading the paper and came across an article about two well-known writers who are married and are cowriting a new book. It started us thinking about how we could work together because we complement each other. Over the following weeks, we mulled over different ideas. We decided to do a series of articles about small villages in Europe and Central America—not just travel pieces but insights into village life, along with information for people who just want to visit. Katherine is doing the research, and I'm doing the writing. She'll do the layout, and I'll edit."

Katherine and Gary have no plans to quit their day jobs, but they are having, as Katherine tags it, "a grand adventure." Gary agrees, "Even if we never sell a single article, it doesn't matter. We enjoy selecting the villages and putting together our travel plans. We've always had great respect for each other, and working together on something benefiting *us* added a deeper dimension to our marriage."

Gary and Katherine's joint venture is an inspiring example of the partnership between two strong individuals who value each other and value being on the same team. When two partners combine their talents, knowledge, and energy, they can achieve things that would be impossible to do alone.

"Love does not consist in gazing at each other," said Antoine de Saint-Exupéry, "but in looking together in the same direction."

VENTURING FORTH

Creating an equal partnership *is* more difficult than letting the man be the boss or giving up and doing all the traditional women's work as well as sharing breadwinning responsibilities. In my seminars, I've heard thousands of women say they feel frustrated by a relationship that is out of sync with the way they want to share their lives with the man they love. In the short run, it *is* simpler to continue to play old familiar roles. But in the long run, it wears thin. We are better off confronting the issues. A woman who initiates changes in her life— and is prepared for the challenges she'll face—is far less likely to suffer the anger and resentment that can build up if she feels powerless in her relationship. Getting prepared means knowing what we are up against when we venture forth to shake up the status quo. In the next chapter, we'll take a closer look at the territory and discover the most effective ways to approach it.

3

THE COURAGE TO MAKE WAVES

The war between the sexes is the only
one in which both sides regularly sleep
with the enemy.

—Quentin Crisp

When we compare our expectations of equal partnership with the partnership we actually have, we stare across a chasm the size of the Grand Canyon. We've worked hard; we've gained power and influence in the workplace. Now we look homeward and are disappointed by what we see. Our efforts to be dealt with as an equal make little impression on our partner.

But what can we do? If we speak out and say something men don't want to hear, they get defensive. And the alternative to speaking out—holding our tongue and playing the non-threatening woman—feeds into the sense of powerlessness that already may be too pervasive a factor in our lives.

Nothing has brought women's dilemma to the surface more effectively than the movie *Thelma & Louise,* a feminist fable that rang a carillon of bells in the collective female psyche all across the country. For one splendid moment, feminism was two wild women careening around in a turquoise Thunderbird, drinking tequila and causing mayhem among an assortment of rednecks, police, and sundry other males. Women stood up and cheered while men squirmed in their seats, wondering what was going on.

What was going on is still going on. Although we try to mask it, many women resent men. We even resent the men we love, in spite of our facade of optimism about our relationships with them. What is it about men that we resent? It's the way they act. They are oblivious to the obvious: we have had it with being treated like a junior partner. We expect more from men and want a lot more power in our relationships than we are getting. But often we hit a blank wall. Rightly or wrongly, women really feel that men just don't get it.

Witness the Roper Poll, which found between 70 and 80 percent of men pleased with everything from "how mate helps around house" to "amount of time spent thinking about family responsibilities." Consider that most men (75 percent) say they are happy with their lives and feel that marriage is terrific. (Eighty-eight percent say they would marry the same woman again.)

The very same poll found women seething! At least half of them feel "resentful" (that word again) about the identical issues, "fed up," and even "angrier at men than they were twenty years ago." It may not be a full-blown grudge that women bear toward men, but it isn't exactly a feeling of goodwill. The poll concluded that women are now far less likely to view men as kind, gentle, and thoughtful, and far more likely to see them as selfish, self-centered, and uninterested in their home life.

Women are tired of fighting the same skirmishes again and again with their lovers over equal partnership. They feel stymied about what to do next. After all, there are limits on our options for resolving disputes with our partner. For starters, we can't fire him or put him on probation. But we aren't entirely without resources. We know a lot about managing difficult people and situations on the job, and we can learn to put this knowledge to better use in our romantic relationships.

First, we have to ask ourselves why it is so difficult for us to initiate changes in our relationship. This means owning up to the fact that, too often, we back away from our anger. We fear it may be a bottomless well, and we are afraid to tap it; we worry about damaging our relationship. We'd do better to stop being so timid about anger and see it as a signal that something has gone haywire and needs to be fixed. And the only way to get things fixed is to make waves—shake up the status quo. *Having the courage to make waves is a necessary requirement to having the kind of equal partnership we want.* This newly found courage frees us to channel our anger and frustration to changing the circumstances of our relationship.

The next step is to understand why men are so slow in adjusting to women's expectations of equality. When I say "understand," I'm not referring to being more empathetic—not that being empathetic isn't worthy. Rather, I'm talking about increasing our awareness of men's perspective and thought processes.

WHAT WOMEN NEED TO KNOW ABOUT MEN'S RESISTANCE

Is examining men's resistance to equality a waste of time? If you think so, you have a lot of company. In my seminars, when I present my belief that we need to be more savvy about men's thinking, women either moan out loud or go into attack mode. We are so impatient with men, we tend to get sullen or sarcastic about a suggestion to spend any more of our energy peering into their psyche. Most women feel they have already spent too much time trying to understand men.

But consider how carefully you would study a potential client, or how much research you would do on a firm you were interested in. Before you hire someone, you screen the applicants, interview them, and get references. These techniques help us get to know who that person really is. For example, look at how Helayne Spivak, the top creative executive with the Young & Rubicam ad agency in New York, learns all she can about her target audience. "In advertising, before we sit down to write a commercial, we go through stacks of research to learn who our audience is. How old are they? Where do they live? What are their buying habits? We look at all other advertising in the category to see what's been done, past and present. We interview consumers to understand what they like and dislike. It's a painstaking process, but when it's over we know whom we're talking to and exactly what to say to them."

Spivak's "study your client" approach is exactly the strategy we have to take if we are ever going to make real progress in becoming equal partners with the men we love. Or if you prefer, you can look at it from another angle. Ellen Belzer, president of Belzer Seminars and Consulting, advocates, "Do your homework." She illustrates her point by telling us about how Margaret Thatcher, before her first meeting with Mikhail Gorbachev in 1984, read every speech by Gorbachev that she could find, talked to dozens of people, and assembled a group of experts for an all-day briefing. As Thatcher noted, "It's rather like a military campaign: Time spent on reconnaissance is seldom wasted."

Ask yourself, do I really know how men today feel about equal partnership with women? After all, it isn't politically correct for men to make disparaging remarks about "women's lib" anymore. They are careful to call it "the women's movement," and pointedly avoid saying, "I'll have my girl call your girl." But could it be that underneath the liberated male exterior beats the heart of a fifties stereotypical man? Is equality between the sexes proceeding so slowly because men have mastered the buzzwords of the nineties liberated male, but are only paying lip-service to parity?

After all, men have long been dominant in our culture. They enjoy a favored position that yields them a major share of the market in money, power, and prestige. Why would they volunteer to give all of it, or even some of it, up? Many scholars, including sociologist William J. Goode of Columbia University, dismiss the notion of a grand plan or conspiracy among men to keep the wealth to themselves. Goode suggests that we look at the "sociology of the dominant group" to understand men's attitudes about women's quest for equality. He explains that men "take for granted the system that gives them their status; they are not aware of how much the social structure, from attitude patterns to laws, pervasively yields small, cumulative, and eventually large advantages in most competitions."

My reading is that men simply don't see the issues surrounding equality the same way women do. For example, you may have noticed that most men, because they feel that they didn't personally create the system, resent and reject the charge that they are somehow responsible for the inequities between the genders. In fact, at my seminars this is always grist for heated debate. Men get very upset at any suggestion that they have had anything to do with women's lack of equality. And women are incredulous that men can dismiss the evidence of inherited male power so blindly.

According to Goode, when men look at the issue, they don't believe they are reaping unearned bonuses and blessings by being male. They are more aware of the burdens and responsibilities they bear than their privileges. Men view even small losses of deference, advantage, or opportunity as large threats, and don't notice their own gains or their maintenance of old advantages.

Although nearly all men have been touched in some way or other by the women's movement, many regard what is happening as something "out there" that has very little relevance to their own lives.

To these men, the movement is a dialogue mainly among women—conferences of women whining about men, a mixture of just or exaggerated complaints, and shrill demands to which men are not obligated to respond unless legally forced.

Now that we've examined the "sociology of the dominant group," let's study another aspect of why our client—our man—acts the way he does. Lurking deep down beneath men's tough exterior is another clue as to why they are so uncomfortable about women's quest for equality. When I listen to a man talk about the swift pace of change in his relationships with women, I hear a shaky voice. Boys grow up taking for granted that what they are, and what they do, is far superior to what girls are and do. Boys believe that where they are is where the action is. Growing up, men get used to basking in the spotlight and expect to have women's attention focused on them. Although high visibility is perilous—it makes one vulnerable to rejection and egg-in-your face failure—it is also ego gratifying and desirable.

Men sense the shift in the cultural wind and feel their star dimming. Women are getting more national attention and becoming more important in the world of politics and economics. Women are finding each other more interesting than in the past, and they're getting more involved in what other women are doing. Work occupies more of their attention. Being without a man for a while does not seem to be such a terrible thing to women anymore. Men simply aren't as omnipresent in women's lives as they once were.

In some worried but unfocused way, men perceive they are losing something by becoming equal partners with women. They say they are relieved not to bear all of the burden of breadwinning; they tell us they like sassy, ambitious women. Yet I think many men—even the most feminist of men—feel threatened by their diminished place in women's hearts and minds, although most would rather walk over a bed of hot coals than admit it. Occasionally a man will talk about his life now that his wife has other interests besides him, and we can hear his wounded howls of displacement loud and clear. For example, a Los Angeles public relations man told Mary Bralove, a reporter for *The Wall Street Journal,* how shaken he was by his wife's indifference to his work after she launched her own real-estate career. One night he asked his wife for her opinion of a press kit that he had spent many hours preparing. "I asked her the next morning if she had looked at it, and she said, 'No.' I was extremely hurt. She had plenty of time if she had wanted to." Another professional man attributed his divorce to his wife's employment. "I could handle Kris's working okay, but I couldn't handle being second in her life."

True, men are now more comfortable about meeting women's demands for equal opportunity and pay in employment. But I believe that what really bothers men, deep down, is having to give up being fussed over and being the designated spokesperson for the rest of us.

It is unrealistic to expect men to shed all their traditional or semitraditional roles easily or without resistance. As one insightful woman wrote me, "Never underestimate the cunning or the staying power of those in positions of privilege." If you work for an organization that is just now beginning to pull its head out of the sand about women's issues, you know how long it takes to implement new policies. It's not all that different in our personal world.

Becoming partners doesn't come easy. Ninety-eight percent of the women in Shere Hite's study, *Women in Love,* reported a need to make basic changes in their marriages. And, like those women, many of us are getting more and more frustrated with trying to implement those changes. "No matter how they scream, plead, or reason with the men they love, the great majority of women have not been able to bring about the changes in their relationships with men they want," reports Hite. Clearly, screaming, pleading, and reasoning haven't gotten us where we want to go. We need to try a new tack. It is understandable to be impatient with men for dragging their feet about equality, but it's important to be strategic about it.

A SENSE OF SELF:
ASSERTIVENESS VERSUS AGGRESSIVENESS

Assertive women ask for what they want;
aggressive women get what they want.
—A woman from a seminar in Philadelphia

When I query the women in my seminars for suggestions about how women can be more successful in achieving their goals—personally and professionally—I can count on a fierce debate erupting over the concepts of aggressive versus assertive.

"Aggressiveness is being too pushy, too demanding and thoughtless about other people's feelings," one woman said. Others add that an aggressive person is "someone who will run right over you," "a selfish person," "coldhearted." On the flip side, an assertive person is defined as a real "mensch," fair-minded, not too hard and not too soft. Clearly, the vast majority of women view aggressiveness as bad and assertiveness as good.

The above definition of *aggressiveness* certainly implies behavior that is neither altogether acceptable nor appropriate in many business and personal situations. But as women discuss the price they have paid for not being assertive enough, the idea of being aggressive in the right situation becomes a little more plausible, and a lot more appealing. "What's wrong with standing up for your rights?" questioned a participant in one of my workshops. "Maybe we have to be aggressive now, and when women have a fair shake in the world, we can return to being assertive."

Researchers tell us that successful business people all share certain personal traits: confidence, creativity, and—no surprise—assertiveness. (It also helps to be brimming over with the ability to make decisions, to happily welcome responsibility, and to be tenacious.) "In the end, success isn't so much a matter of the qualities a woman has, as what she wants," states Madeline Prober, a consultant on women in business. "But, whatever the motivation, for a woman to possess the energy and the ambition to be successful, she must have a strong sense of self."

"Must have a strong sense of self." It sounds like such an easy criterion to meet. Yet for most women it is one of the most difficult of traits to develop. Intellectually, most women I've met agree that having a strong sense of self is a critical factor in women making their mark. But emotionally it's a different story, especially when it comes to their love life. Even among today's smartest, most ambitious women, who are perfectly capable of asserting themselves in the workplace, there are many who hesitate to put forth this robust sense of "I" at home. And this hesitation presents a formidable barrier to women in getting what they want in their intimate partnership. "Without a clear 'I,' we become overly reactive to what the other person is doing to us, or not doing for us," observes psychologist Harriet Goldhor Lerner. "We end up feeling helpless and powerless to define a new position in the relationship."

Because the issues surrounding equal partnership rest so heavily on our ability to bring a clear sense of "I" to the bargaining table, let's take a careful look at why this business of "self" is such a stumbling block for women.

Most women operate in a powerful state of trance—a subconscious Code of Goodness that pervades our relationships, our sense of who we are. Almost all of us were raised to believe that "good women" focus on the needs and expectations of others, and ignore their own. "Put yourself last" is a legacy passed down from mother to daughter, father to daughter. Mothers sacrifice. Wives sacrifice.

The put-yourself-last message is still on the bulletin board, but with a new twist. For example, consider how Diane, the director of a statewide hospital program, regards her situation. "Finding the time to have a personal life isn't easy with the incredible demands of running a hospital. I love to cook, but Steve and I mostly do 'take out.' I rarely see my friends anymore, and as for seeing a movie, forget it. Having kids is definitely on the back burner—I can't imagine finding the time to raise a child. Women have to be willing to sacrifice a lot of things if they want to have serious careers."

When women like Diane talk about sacrificing, they aren't saying that they feel called upon to give up their personal growth or their career on the altar of marriage. They are saying that they accept the situation that women have to "pay the price," that is, give up personal time and leisure activities, hobbies, and so forth, in order to keep up with the pace of a demanding job.

Because sacrifice of self now is couched in terms of a pragmatic career strategy of "doing what is necessary to get ahead," today's ambitious women are unaware that they are participating in a charade. We aren't expected to give up our career for love and family anymore, but we are still being sold a bill of ill-fitting goods. Men have long been expected to give it their all on their rise to the top of the corporate pyramid. But the expectation of men's sacrifice of their personal life is not comparable to women's in degree or in kind.

Men take it for granted that they don't have to forgo the pleasure of a full-fledged personal life in order to enjoy professional success. In fact, they expect to have a loving family and a comfortable home to provide a safe harbor from the cold world of competition on the job. And they expect to participate in sports and do other activities—play golf, cheer for their favorite football team, work out at the gym—whatever interests them.

How can women achieve the same sense of entitlement that men are born with?

A good place to begin is by psychologically distancing ourselves from the teaching that a woman's career and happy home must exact a pound of her soul. Without a clear, whole, and separate "I" in our lives, it's too easy to fall into the trap of being the one expected to place personal needs last. When we ourselves accept the judgment that a career woman has to abandon the fringe benefits of a personal life—leisure time, hobbies, movies—in order to stay on the career fast track, we are allowing men to define our lives, just as women have allowed men to define their lives for generations. That is a chilling thought indeed. So whenever you feel guilty for asserting yourself and putting your needs on the front burner, stop and take a minute to examine the reasons why. Accept that it is difficult to give up decades of training in selflessness. No one learns to walk, ride a bicycle, or drive a car on the first attempt. It will take some stops and starts before you are able to negotiate a better balanced partnership with your mate.

According to Harriet Goldhor Lerner, good techniques for moving up the selfhood scale include:

- acknowledging both our strengths and our vulnerabilities;
- making clear statements about our beliefs, values, and priorities, and then keeping our behavior congruent with these;
- staying emotionally connected to significant others even when things get pretty intense; and
- addressing difficult and painful issues and taking a stand on matters important to us.

Of course, having a clear sense of self involves more than this, but it's a good start. And that's all it is—a start. You don't simply decide to "have a self" and *presto,* there it is. It takes real work. The effort it takes becomes apparent when you try to carry out the tasks listed above. It is amazing how quickly your old reluctance to make waves reappears. But as you grow more certain in your understanding of the dynamics of self, the process gets easier.

No matter how you feel about the issue of assertiveness versus aggressiveness, let's agree that we do have to rid ourselves of our fears of shaking up the status quo. One of my favorite lessons about how to do just that comes from Jean Baer's classic book, *How to Be an Assertive, Not Aggressive, Woman.* Ms. Baer lets us in on the moment of her "assertiveness breakthrough" that perfectly illustrates how the change of one simple behavior can set off a chain reaction.

First, a little background. Jean, like so many of us, was taught that a good wife puts a hot meal on the table every night. "And I always did, even though I got up at six and worked all day at a very demanding job.

"One Friday I came home after a particularly taxing day at my office, took one look at that mangy chicken in the refrigerator, went upstairs, took a bubble bath, and retired with a highball and a good spy story. Herb arrived some time later, took a look at me, and inquired with concern, 'Are you sick?'

"I answered, 'I feel fine. I just don't want to cook tonight. You have a choice. There's a chicken. You can cook it. You can order in. Or we can go out. I'm not doing anything.'

"He applauded ('Thank God, you're not playing martyr again!'), and took me out to dinner."

Like Baer, once we get a little more willing to risk giving offense to our spouse and a lot less willing to put up with outmoded expectations about women, we'll be freer to be assertive about what we need and want in our partnership.

Let's now examine the trigger points that create anger in our intimate relationship, and find ways to use the same techniques at home that we use at work to effectively channel our frustration and anger.

HOW *NOT* TO MANAGE ANGER

We either make ourselves miserable or we make ourselves strong. The amount of work is the same.

—Carlos Castaneda, *Journey to Ixtlan*

We all have close encounters with some kind of anger on any typical workday. We disagree with a coworker about a project and lose control while arguing for our point of view. A colleague storms into our office seething when she's denied a promotion she felt she deserved.

A client hasn't returned a critical phone call for two days, and our emotions accelerate from annoyance to indignation.

All of our angry reactions to frustrating situations in the workplace can be translated to the dynamics of that fiery emotion in our personal relationships as well. But there is one notable difference: we are far more irrational within marriage than we are outside it. Psychiatrist A. G. Thompson, M.D., of the Tavistock Institute of Marital Studies in London, explains why. "In the depths of our minds we never, throughout all our lives, succeed in freeing ourselves fully from the hates and resentments that first arose in infancy, or from the excessive and unreal demands and expectations of those earliest years. These emotional forces are part of the essential dynamics of our personalities, and they operate intensely in marriage as they do in any emotional relationship, and lead inevitably to some measure of conflict, frustration and aggressive reaction against the partner."

In other words, the closer we get to another person, the more our unresolved internal conflicts are likely to surface. We let out our "craziness"—our unresolved inner conflicts—in the safety of our most intimate relationships. Most of us would say that we don't consciously ignore the principles of fair play when interacting with our lover. Yet if we are honest with ourselves, we have to admit that there are times when we deal with the person we are closest to very differently than we deal with our colleagues at work.

What happens when we are angry but can't express our feelings to our mate? In sheer frustration, we may assert ourselves by resorting to a stratagem that has the shadowy characteristics of guerrilla warfare—retreat, hide, strike, and vanish. Instead of confronting the issue, we mutter under our breath, throw a sarcastic remark in his general direction, slam the door as we exit the room, refuse to acknowledge his presence.

Sonya, who directs the consumer finance division of a home mortgage company, explains how she changed her style of communicating with her spouse when she realized that her tactics were self-defeating. "Joel likes to have everything in its place and has a specific place for everything. I have to be so precise at the office, I like to kick back when I get home. One Saturday he suggested we clean up the kitchen. I was less than enthused, but he got up to his elbows in it, emptying cupboards and scrubbing the shelves. When he began to put all my spices in alphabetical order and line up cans and boxes, I became indignant. I do all the cooking; the kitchen is my turf—even if it is all out of order. I let him know how upset I felt by stomping in and out of the room and growling in his general direction. He didn't notice. He was so engrossed in his merry little task that I went upstairs, as much to reduce the temptation to hit him over the head with a blunt object as to catch up on some paperwork.

"I came across a memo that I had sent to an employee confirming an agreement we had discussed at a meeting. It was one tough meeting. She had nearly ruined a project that I had worked for months on. Even though I felt like lashing out at her, I didn't. But I wanted her to know that her behavior was not appropriate. I never raised my voice but relied on 'hot' words to convey the message—words such as 'I'm indignant, flabbergasted, deeply disappointed . . .' Things were tense, but we outlined a course of action to insure that it wouldn't happen again (hence the memo).

"I realized that my sulking was a lot less effective than honestly dealing with anger. I marched downstairs and calmly but forcefully told Joel how I felt about his intruding upon *my* kitchen. His view was that he was just contributing his fair share of housekeeping and doing a task he knew I wouldn't like to do. 'Besides,' he said, 'why didn't you just say something?' Although this could have been one of those disagreements where we both go to our battle stations, we didn't. And by being straightforward with each other we were able to move on to discussing the real issues: too much control and too little assertiveness." Once Sonya understood how she related to Joel, she was freer to deal with the real grievance that had caused her ire, just as she did when she had a problem with her employees.

When you learn to manage anger, it no longer has power over you. This means confronting the problem directly rather than wallowing in wounded feelings or slinking around in the jungle.

Using guerrilla tactics to get back at our spouse for something he has done, or not done, does us more harm than good. While such behavior may give women some temporary, superficial victories in the battle of the sexes, they come at a very high cost. Guerrilla tactics chip away at our self-confidence because they are signals that we aren't taking control of our lives.

CONTROLLING ANGER

Kathryn Stechert Black, who writes about women and the world of work, believes that whether we are at the office or at home we are either a manager or a victim of anger. "When we are facing the bad behavior of someone out of control—a spouse bellowing out his rancor, or the legitimate gripe of a good employee—the best response is to stand up to the anger. That doesn't mean getting angry back; it means taking a calm, deliberate approach. If you get defensive, you won't resolve a thing."

Diana, who manages a major Santa Fe art gallery, agrees. She has found that the best way to cope with a blustery person is to stay in control and not shrink from the situation. "There are times when I have to stand up for myself and take a strong stand, just to show I'm in charge. Artists can be temperamental to work with and they try to intimidate you. You can't act like a wimp or they won't respect you. But you can't get into a shouting match with them either. I stay matter-of-fact and expect them to get their act together."

Diana applies the same calm-in-a-storm technique when things get high-pitched between she and her spouse, Michael. "Both of us tend to have a short fuse," she explains, "and I try to remind myself that losing my temper sets off a chain reaction. I've learned the most effective thing I can do is to remain in control. I may say 'I'm upset about (whatever).' I don't mince words, but I carefully choose them. I try not to resort to threats or name calling and be alert to what is making me so angry so I can do something about it."

We can't always avoid conflict, but like Diana, we can channel our anger in ways that don't inflict damage on ourselves, our spouses, or anyone else. Although we may have a difficult time being assertive, we can still pick the best moment to let our partner know what we're feeling. Margaret, assistant vice president of a Chicago-area bank, states, "It's important to know when to say, 'Now listen! This makes me very angry, and I won't allow you to do it again.' But I always, always remain in control. I communicate my displeasure quietly at first and raise my voice only if I'm not getting a response. This is more effective than ranting and raving."

At the office, we know that uncontrolled outbursts win us only ridicule and disdain: no one can be articulate while having a tantrum. Not only could we be accused of overacting or being childish, our status would be instant pariah. On an effectiveness scale, we rate that stratagem a zero.

There is an old saying that when couples fight fire with fire, they end up in ashes. There are times when any of us is susceptible to spontaneous combustion. The unfortunate reality is that no matter how angry we are, it's hard to justify having a temper fit and lashing out at a colleague or our partner. It's not okay to just ventilate and agitate, we have to fix the circumstances that make us angry in the first place.

CHANNELING ANGER

The flip side of ventilating anger—suppressing it in order to preserve our marriage—is just as harmful. There is a wise Chinese proverb: "Anger eats away the vessel that contains it."

Judith found this out on her second honeymoon. For two hectic weeks prior to the trip, she worked overtime to meet the deadline for a major foundation grant. Judith is a fund-raiser, and getting that grant was a life-and-death issue for her agency. She made it, got the grant package over to Federal Express, and headed for home to throw some things in a suitcase and take off on a long-awaited getaway with her spouse, Bill.

Numb with relief and excited about going away for what promised to be a romantic interlude, she swung open her front door and walked straight into "a royal mess." That morning Bill, who had taken the day off, had promised to straighten up, pack the cooler, and have everything ready to go. What did she find? Bill watching a tennis tournament on television. When he saw her, "he had the same look a deer gets when caught in the headlights."

"I was infuriated," Judith recalls. "But I knew that if I popped off with how I really felt he would get defensive and we would get into an argument. I so wanted a great vacation together, I tried to just be a good sport and pitch in with the chores. But I couldn't shake off my irritation with him, and it ruined the weekend for me. I haven't really gotten over it yet."

Judith, like many other women, suffers from battle fatigue. After a day at the office putting out fires and shuffling papers, who wants to come home and get into an argument? "This is a huge issue for many women who have not learned how to express what they want or need," explains psychologist Barbara Brown. "Women can feel really lost when they have to assert their position and get specific on an issue. Much depression and anger and resentment are internalized because they can't speak up on their own behalf."

But sooner or later our feelings surface in one way or another. "Unexpressed anger can fuel deeper resentment," notes Ann, a trial lawyer in South Carolina. "I specialize in family law, and I see how petty arguments blow up. People bicker over something minor until it becomes a matter of principle not to give in. Some couples have the silliest reasons for divorce . . . That's the most important lesson I've brought home from work: not to let petty grievances interfere with my love for my family."

To better handle our grievances—petty or not, assertively or aggressively—we have to speak up on our own behalf at home, just as we do at the office. We become ineffective and fuzzy agents of change if we ourselves aren't clear about what we expect of our partner and what we expect of ourselves. As Oscar Wilde cautioned, "When the gods wish to punish us they answer our prayers."

Stella Resnick, Ph.D., a well-known therapist in private practice in Los Angeles, advises, "Take the time to unearth your real thoughts and feelings. Your surface reactions may not be the most accurate. Make a list of what you expect to happen. Put it all down—deeper expectations as well as everyday wishes."

After you've gotten a clear picture of what it is that you want to see happen, you'll need to express your feelings to your mate. Resnick gives us courage to be direct: "In a relationship of two people, each person has the right to make rules, each person has the right to ask for what they need and want from the other person. You have to lay it all out—your dreams, your hopes, your fears. Take a deep breath. Exhale. Let your lover know exactly what it is that you are feeling."

Maria, the owner of an employee leasing agency, took Resnick's advice and put it into action. In her words, "One of the reasons I am an entrepreneur is that I hate having a boss. I like the challenge of taking a risk and getting the reward. I'll go to the mat with anyone to compete for a company's business. But in my personal life I tend to back off.

"Joe and I have been married two years, and over the last year I've found myself annoyed when he began to cross the line from caring to bossiness. He told me what looked good on me, what was worth watching on TV, how to handle my accountant. I thought it was kind of sweet when we were first married, but I resent getting advice I don't seek or, frankly, want. The turning point came at a dinner party. The host asked me what I wanted to drink and, before I could respond, Joe gave him my order without even a nod in my direction. Then, when I reached for an canape, he pointed to the one I should take. I wanted to shout at him, 'Mother, I want to do it myself.' It was awful. I was so angry I worried that I would blurt out the wrong thing and do damage to our relationship.

"Then, I got inspired. I remembered the time my assistant had become so overly solicitous he was driving me crazy. What did I do? I followed the advice of one of my business teachers years ago: 'Focus on solving the problem, not on assessing blame.' I met with my assistant and gently let him know how uncomfortable I felt about unsolicited advice. I spelled out what kind of advice I welcomed and what kind I did not. He was upset at first and tiptoed around me for a few days. I felt edgy myself. Eventually we got comfortable again about working together, and now we get along just fine.

"When Joe and I got home that night after the party, I discussed the problem just as I had done with my assistant. Art was surprised and hurt because I had managed to put on such a false happy face. He accused me of being dishonest. It took every ounce of my communication skills to use 'I' statements and not venture off on a 'You' blaming tangent. Things are so much better now, I only wish I had done it sooner. I do appreciate Joe's concern and value his advice. I just don't need so much of it."

CONQUERING THE NEED FOR APPROVAL WITH THE "SO WHAT" APPROACH

"Autonomy simply isn't a value that society encourages in women," comments Dr. Anne Jardim, coauthor of *The Managerial Woman*. "I'm thinking of a sense of independence, a clear sense of identity, very clear, very strong." Nor does our society approve of women who make waves.

Too often this social disapproval for women who show a strong sense of self intimidates us because we fear that we will offend or put someone off. I've had to laugh at how Mary Kay Blakely describes the limits we put on ourselves. "Ours is the first revolution in history that requires its proponents to foment change without hurting anyone's feelings." To remedy this, we need to keep alert to whether we are being overly sensitive to those critics who prefer meek women.

Take the case of Hillary Clinton, the wife of President Bill Clinton. During the presidential campaign, she was criticized and sniped at although she epitomizes a woman of the nineties: a competent and caring person, the kind of woman we would like our daughters to become. Patricia O'Brien, in the summer before the presidential election, profiled her for *Working Woman* magazine. "She is," reported O'Brien, "a woman who is a lawyer, an advocate for children, a director on several corporate boards and a conscientious mother. In person she isn't intimidating. She eats popcorn like a kid and greets a good joke with a wonderful belly laugh." But she projects something that men find unsettling.

For example, O'Brien points to former president Richard Nixon who declared, "Hillary pounds the piano so hard that Bill can't be heard. You want a wife who's intelligent, but not too intelligent." "What, then, is she supposed to be?" asks O'Brien.

There was a time when I would have just read along, seeking an answer from the article, anxious to know what she *is* supposed to be. But now I've learned a way to put that kind of disapproval into a new perspective. We women must stand back and assess the criticism. If it has some merit, we can learn from it. If it is without merit, we need to challenge it. It's too easy to retreat to a self-doubt cave when we fear offending other women, or if men (including our beloved) might find our self-assurance unsettling. In effect, the best way to deal with criticism is to apply a test to the situation. Ask yourself, "So what?" So Nixon thinks a man ought to have a not-too-intelligent wife. So what? Just because someone doesn't appreciate a competent, outspoken woman, it doesn't mean she's suspect or wrong. Why should this kind of carping about feminist women bother us? Or Hillary Clinton, for that matter?

This "so-what?" approach is one I've adapted from the seminars on risk-taking and leadership offered at Larry Wilson's Pecos River Training Center, a company that specializes in corporate team-building training. A fundamental tenet of this approach is to be open and confident, not dismissive or overly negative. The theory doesn't suggest that nothing can be learned from criticism. Rather, it is a way to challenge yourself to take risks, no matter what others may think of you. If, for example, you launched a campaign to sell zillions of widgets, and you sold zilch, can you deal with the consequences? You could go broke. You could be ridiculed for your poor decisions. You could be shunned by your peers. If you aren't able to stare down those negatives and say, "So what?" you need to decide on another course of action.

To succeed in business, there will be times when you have to deal with the consequences of taking a risk or not taking a risk. We can apply these same basic principles to help us sort out risk-taking ventures in our intimate relationship. When you are at a decision-making crossroads, make a list of all the potential consequences of each action you could take. Then apply the test: imagine dealing with each of those consequences by challenging yourself to honestly answer the question, "So what?" You may discover that certain actions could have too negative a fallout, or you may find that you are capable of dealing with whatever happens.

The "So what?" test is a thoughtful exercise to encourage you to make better judgments about what should influence your actions and what you can safely ignore. The point is to avoid letting some vague sense of public approval keep us trapped in the same old cycle of inequality.

Naturally, it would be unrealistic to contend that other people's approval of us is *never* important. Long-term career success depends not only on good performance but on the positive perceptions other people have of you. At least half of the women executives responding to a survey by *Working Woman* magazine stated that a key factor in their success was a high approval rating, along with being considered "smart and having an impressive image." Also important was their ability to work with others, their knack for adapting to the business environment, and their gracious, relaxed, and genuine demeanor.

On the home front, we desire high approval ratings just as we do at the office. We want our spouse, family, and friends to think well of us and approve of the way we handle ourselves. The problem arises when our sense of worth depends too much upon the approval of others, to the extent that when it's not forthcoming we feel anxious and inadequate.

Paula, a corporate manager of an employee assistance program, offers her version of the "So what?" method for distinguishing between criticism that has merit and criticism that doesn't. "When I am upset by disapproving 'comments' or 'suggestions' other people make about a project I'm working on, I try not to instantly take them to heart. I try to get all the information I can about why they feel the way they do and then determine whether or not their criticism has merit. I find a quiet place to consider what was said, and consider the context in which it was said. Sometimes others are right; sometimes they aren't. If I think their comments are helpful, I gratefully thank them. If I determine that their understanding of the project is off base, I try to clear it up. But I don't take their criticism personally. So what? It's simply their opinion versus mine. No more; no less. I've tried to transfer that same attitude to my home life."

Besides her job, Paula copes with the demands of two children and evening business classes. She describes how she deals with approval for her choices about her life:

"Do I take flak from relatives, 'friends,' the people at my daughter's school, and total strangers about neglecting my family for my own pursuits? You bet I do. Do I sometimes feel guilty? Definitely. Would I have it any other way? Not on your life."

Paula evaluated her situation, examined the reaction of others to juggling her career and family, and decided she could live with the consequences of not getting universal approval. We all crave approval, but we have to accept the fact that we won't get everyone's nod of permission for the choices we make about our lives.

Unfortunately, having the courage to speak up on our own behalf is no guarantee of instant bliss on the home front. Things may get tense, maybe even *very* tense, between you and your partner. And that's not a point to be taken lightly. When a woman begins to define herself in terms of her own life and then initiates new role expectations—not only for herself but for her partner—she risks being called "selfish," "ungiving," or, more cruelly, "a bitch." But this is extreme. Most of the time, two people manage to work through the tension and adjust to the changes.

Roxanne, the co-owner of a florist shop, had to make a decision to make waves and assert herself in her partnership or drown. She recalls, "Last year after Christmas, I needed a vacation, I was a frazzled mess. I told my husband, Mel, I had to get away. Before I could bring up some options, Mel just cut the discussion off with, 'I can't get off work, we'll have to go in the summer.' I didn't pursue it, as I didn't want to get into an argument. I was too tired to argue. I thought about what to do—soften him up by bringing home travel brochures?

"But after a few days I began to think about why I hadn't been more assertive. The problem? I tend to not argue back with Mel. He has a strong personality and sometimes overwhelms me. He doesn't mean to come off as a bully, but he has a very adamant way of expressing himself. Maybe because I felt the need so strongly, or because I finally realized that it was time for me to speak up, I took stock of how I handle differences of opinion at the shop. I wouldn't just blurt out to my partner: 'I gotta get out of here!' I would discuss the situation and we would work things out. That is a lot easier said than done. She has the same kind of strong personality that Mel has. But, as her business partner, I learned a long time ago not to back down. If we don't agree, I certainly don't slink away. And I don't expect that we will like each other's point of view all of the time. I do expect that we will take each other's needs seriously and try to meet them. This strategy has worked great for us for years: our business is solid and we have a terrific relationship.

"That night, I was direct with Mel and told him I understood that he couldn't get away for a vacation. But I could and I needed to recharge my batteries now, not later. Even if he was unhappy about it, I told him I had to do what I had to do. I was firm, as I am with Ruth, but open to a discussion of the options. What a difference—he listened and understood that I was serious. I ended up going with my good friend Barbara for two weeks, and Mel joined us for a long weekend. He didn't much like the idea of me going away without him. You can't please other people all the time. You can't in business, and you can't in marriage. It's sounds corny, but as my favorite Ricky Nelson song goes, 'Sometimes you gotta please yourself.'"

Like Roxanne, you can break away from the binds of intimidation by carefully examining those encounters that cause you to feel unsure of yourself. Try to stay impartial and distance yourself psychologically from the intensity of the situation. Focus on your goals. And be prepared to deal with the consequences of your partner's reactions.

A good role model for how to handle a measure of predictable crankiness on the part of our mate when we assert ourselves is a woman I've never even met but admire. In an article that's one of my favorites, author W. W. Meade describes his reaction to his wife's assertiveness with unusual honesty:

The person with whom I share a marriage just interrupted me. It made me testy. She knew it would. I know she
knew because she did not come into my studio but stood
outside the window to ask me a question. Now, in the
old days I would have been kind about it and later taken
it out on her or the kid or the cats. I would have thought
her frail for needing to interrupt me and thought of
myself as strong for enduring it.

These days it seems clear that she knew I would
not like it, yet she risked that because she wanted to do
her work and did not want the unanswered thing hang-
ing over her. Her work matters to her, and she will sometimes let it have overriding importance.

What appeals to me so much about this woman is that she knew
her spouse would get upset when she asserted herself and *she did it
anyway.* And the payoff is that he has a newfound respect for her.

There are times when it is tempting to just forget about trying
to achieve a more equal intimate relationship. From a distance, a traditional marriage looks so cozy, so secure, so free from the constant
haggling over equality. When you find yourself feeling that way, try to
remember that it is an illusion. "Traditional relationships are like junk
food," explains psychologist Harriet Goldhor Lerner, "they always
remain the same, and eventually poison you. A transitional relationship between a man and a woman may not look as good because it is
filled with the overt expression of the conflicts experienced by two
people who are open with each other and are trying to achieve a satisfying, dynamic balance—as opposed to the pseudopeace of traditional
relationships where the emphasis is on [being] nice and understanding while suppressing the negative."

Working out equality between men and women means a bit of
stormy weather, but it's never boring.

ANGER AS A CATALYST

Getting angry over the slow pace of change in social parity and equal opportunity, in both our public and private lives, isn't all bad. After all, these emotions were the prime movers behind the fight for civil rights and the women's movement. "There are times when only anger will make the necessary point," says author Carol Tavris, "when gentle hints and persistent kindnesses go unheard and unheeded by the irritating spouse or government in question." Indeed, the power of anger can be the catalyst for men and women to finally negotiate a truce.

"If you always do what you've always done, you will always get what you've always gotten." Walking through the conference room of the Pecos River Training Center that poster caught my eye and stopped me in my tracks. If we don't like what we are getting in our intimate partnership, we'll have to do things differently than we've done—such as confronting our anger.

In fact, women are benefiting by acknowledging that anger does have a place in their lives. "We are being strengthened by it," confirms Marcia Appel, executive director of the Association of Area Business Publications. "Our anger before was ideological. Now it's based on real experiences. But that's good, because we're now more likely to do more to change the problem."

It's not always easy to discriminate between the sources of anger that you can do something about and those you can't. There is a big difference, for example, between the events surrounding us that we can personally change through our own actions, and those situations that are beyond our control. "Nowadays," writes feminist author Jane O'Reilly, "I divide the blame more equitably: half for me and half for societal arrangements." That is a wise attitude for any woman to adopt.

*　　*　　*

In our valiant efforts to hurry along the process of being equal partners, we've tried bribing our beloved, cajoling him, sulking, guerrilla
warfare—everything short of hitting him on the head with a
saucepan. However, as this chapter showed us, those tactics are not
only wearying, they are ineffective. Now let's move ahead and look at
an overall strategy that will enable us to settle conflict and cut a new
deal with our partner—negotiation.

4

THE GENTLE ART
OF NEGOTIATION

Let us never negotiate out of fear, but
let us never fear to negotiate.
—John F. Kennedy

The Rolling Stones had it right—you can't always get what you want. Worse, most of us have a hard time even asking for what we want. "Yet others quietly, charmingly, and smoothly manage to ask for what they want without getting anxious or angry," observes Janet Horton, a management consultant. "They also don't back down the minute an opponent resists, or give away the store. They know how to negotiate."

Negotiate? Does it feel crude to utter the word *negotiate* in the same breath with words about our romantic relationship? After all, we cut our teeth on tales of the magic of true love, of how lovers who really love each other communicate without words, how they willingly sacrifice to please the other. Love conquers all. As charming as the notion of lover's ESP is, alas, it is a figment of the romance novelist's imagination. If love conquered all, we wouldn't find half of all marriages ending in divorce, and Dear Abby would go out of business.

Of course partners love each other, but we can't rely on love to solve every difference of opinion about leisure time, careers, money, or even sex. The fact that we inevitably have conflicts isn't the real issue. The real issue is how well we handle the disputes that are bound to surface in working and living with other people. Author Michael Korda gives us this insight: "Love gives us the patience, the desire, the determination to sustain the relationship, but the details have to be worked out with a sense of fairness, equality, and self-respect."

Consider the case of the lark and the nightingale. Marilyn is a physician and Dan, her spouse, a middle school teacher. She describes herself as "a morning person, a lark." Dan, on the other hand, likes to stay up late. "I'm a nightingale," he says. The problem? Marilyn couldn't function without a good night's rest and required a quiet, dark room to get to sleep. In order for Dan to fall asleep, he had to read in bed. Going into another room and reading until he was sleepy didn't count; he had to be in his bed. They argued off and on for the first three years of their marriage about who got to decide when the lights went out. Each had gone off to sleep on the couch—sometimes in anger, sometimes to keep the peace. But a separate sleeping space for each wasn't a satisfying solution because they liked the coziness of waking up next to each other. The situation grated more on Marilyn. "He could sleep through an earthquake!" she contends. But when she realized how cranky and dysfunctional she was at work without a solid night's rest, she knew they had to find a way to resolve the issue, short of divorce.

It's not that Marilyn is without experience in dealing with tough situations. "My days are full of give-and-take and making decisions," she tells me. "I've taken several continuing education courses on how to handle difficult people and testy situations through negotiation. It seems natural to me to be up front about what I want to see happen in my professional life, but applying negotiation skills at home seems artificial or manipulative somehow."

Finally, in desperation, Marilyn decided to stop complaining and solve the problem in a straightforward way. She recalls, "One early evening before we went to bed I asked Dan to discuss how we could deal with our unmatched sleep patterns. After some lengthy back-and-forth we came to an agreement. If he wanted to read past ten o'clock (a negotiated lights-out) he would use a reading light, and I would use a sleeping mask."

This first solution didn't work, however. Marilyn could hear him turning the pages in the book. (As a fellow light sleeper I know she's not crazy.) She couldn't rest because she knew that most nights he eventually nods off with the book clutched in his hands and the reading light on. She had to take his hands off the book and turn off the light (he never blinked an eye) before she could really get to sleep. It was back to the drawing board.

The next experiment is the one that took. She wears a sleeping mask ("call me the Lone Ranger") and ear plugs and lets him fend for himself if he falls asleep with book in hand. He turns out the lights at eleven o'clock, sleepy or not. If not, he goes into another room to read.

One of the best things Marilyn and Dan did was *not* to try to arrive at a perfect solution. Wisely, they knew it wasn't possible. They took the most effective approach by seeking a practical not-quite-perfect-but-satisfying solution that both could live with. They tried one thing, and when that didn't work they invented something else. A key to their success was defining their conflict as a *mutual* problem and concentrating on a common goal (living and sleeping together in harmony). They recognized that everyone has individual quirks about the conditions they need to fall asleep. You simply can't will a nightingale into a lark or vice versa. So why resort to blaming or name calling? Because they treated each other so well, so gently, they were able to concentrate on the real issue—they had a problem that needed fixing and together they set out to fix it.

Without putting a label to it, Marilyn and Dan practiced a classic form of negotiation: Win-win. Not give-gain. "The goal of many hard-nosed business executives is to win, implying that the other guy loses," states physician and novelist Francis Roe. "But they don't love their competitors. When you are negotiating with the person you live with and love, you have a vested interest in being certain that they don't feel defeated." Hence, the fundamental aim of win-win negotiation is for the people on both sides of the bargaining table to walk away as winners. The major difficulty, and opportunity, is that the deal struck must benefit both sides so that both sides are invested in making it work.

It is a tightrope, but it is walkable. Professionals who handle disputes and conflict resolution—marriage counselors, lawyers, mediators, and others who teach negotiation skills or who negotiate for a living—promise that anyone can improve their negotiation skills. "Winning negotiators," declares Gerald Nierenberg, author of *The Complete Negotiator,* "are trained, not born." On those encouraging words, let's look at simple but effective win-win negotiation principles.

TIGERS NEED NOT APPLY

When you think it is a jungle out there, it becomes a jungle.
—Gerald Nierenberg, author

One of the most articulate advocates of win-win negotiating is Larry Wilson, founder of the Pecos River Training Center in Pecos, New Mexico. His philosophy is that unless both parties are committed to the idea that both will be winners, he won't even begin to negotiate.

The agreed-upon goal of both people, right from the outset, has to be that neither will lose.

At the core of win-win negotiation is bargaining, that is, trading something you have for something someone else has that you want. There is only so much of each commodity—time, energy, money—in a relationship. Each person wants a fair share of those commodities. But don't expect to receive the same exact percentage of the resources each day, week, or year. We have to develop some sort of exchange in which we agree for one person to get more goodies sometimes and the other to get more goodies at other times. Keeping an exact score leads to needless fights over increasingly trivial issues.

In business and in love, negotiating a deal where everyone wins is a fine art that requires two key skills. One is collaboration; the other is compromise.

Collaboration means that you both see a problem as one that can be resolved by making sure each of you gets a fair share, rather than by expecting one or both of you to sacrifice something or take a loss. You collaborate by working out a deal to make more pie so that each of you can have a bigger piece. For example, you know that in two weeks the draft of a big-bucks grant proposal will land on your desk and you'll be responsible for getting it out fast. You could simply announce this fact to your assistant and expect him to work overtime as needed even though you know that he hates to work under pressure. Or you could collaborate by asking him how he'd like to go about meeting the deadline to avoid burning the midnight oil. Together you can collaborate on a way to ease the pain—take off an extra day before things get heated up, start now to prepare the completed sections of the draft that are already okayed, hire temporary help, and so forth.

"Collaboration takes time and trust," advises Pat Heim, author of *Hardball for Women*. "To have a meaningful discussion you must both care about your underlying concerns, be willing to understand each other, and be open to influence."

Compromise—the second key negotiation skill—is not anyone's favorite strategy. As counselor Terry Beresford describes it, "Compromise is that knot in your stomach when you don't get your way." Because we do like to get our way, we often wish (secretly or out loud) that the other person would graciously volunteer to give in to prove his love. Or we get tired of making the kind of effort necessary to work out a compromise. As Rachel, a woman I interviewed, complained, "The thing I dislike the most about being married is compromise, compromise. Sometimes I'm so busy and so preoccupied that I would like not to have to invest energy in discussing everything with him."

Despite its shortcomings, compromise can be a useful fallback position from which to negotiate an acceptable-to-good deal when you simply aren't coming up with any creative solutions. Compromise means trading concessions; the seller wants $100, you want to pay $80, you compromise at $90. Or you trade choices. Janis and Hal plan a Friday night out—dinner and a movie—but they have different ideas about what they want to eat and see. Hal wants to see an action-adventure film; Janis wants to see a comedy. Hal wants to eat at a Mexican cafe; Janis prefers Indian food. So they compromise: one of them chooses the movie and the other, the restaurant.

True, when you compromise, both sides end up with less than they wanted. But 90 percent of something is better than 100 percent of nothing. And it's better to have a loving relationship than score a massive victory.

The most vital rule of compromise is that neither person gives up something he or she will regret. In other words, don't give away the life raft, just the parts you don't need to stay afloat. Expect your partner to do the same thing, and you both come out ahead.

The strategies of collaboration and compromise, when used with the principles of win-win negotiation, allow us to transfer conflict-resolution skills from our job to our personal life. The rest of the this chapter deals with the do's and don'ts of productive negotiating. As we'll learn, even the most savvy negotiator in the business world can have trouble negotiating her own needs at home.

GET YOUR PRIORITIES STRAIGHT

When we settle in to negotiate, we need to pay as much attention to our relationship with the other person as to the issue being negotiated. You have to separate the problem from what's going on between you and your partner. "Remember," advises psychologist Barbara Brown, "your partner isn't out to hurt you because his wants and needs are different from yours. To disagree doesn't mean not to love." Adding to this point, negotiators Roger Fisher and Scott Brown give us this warning: "You can't buy a good relationship by making concessions in a negotiation, nor will a relationship work well if you try to extort concessions in a negotiation as a condition for keeping the relationship alive."

An intimate partnership is a cooperative venture, not a competitive battle. It's important to avoid the adversarial relationship that exists in most business deals; the establishment of joint goals is a vital prerequisite for negotiating.

Often we find ourselves falling into the trap of arguing like a lawyer, convinced that we are right and that it's only a matter of time before our "opponent" sees the light and admits defeat. Part of the reason lawyers are good at bargaining is that they are dealing with other people's problems; they don't plan on having breakfast with either their client or the opposing side for many mornings thereafter. But even a courtroom lawyer, if she's wise, puts win-win strategies to work. She, more than anyone, knows how to use these strategies to get what she wants—to charm the hostile witness, win over the jury, maintain the respect of opposing counsel (who may be assigned to her side on the next case). Even the most aggressive attorney doesn't want to risk alienating the opposition *too* much; she wants to keep alive the option of winning them over to her side.

Jimmy Calano and Jeff Salzman, president and vice president of Career Track, a seminar company, learned this lesson when they were involved in a tough lawsuit settlement. The opposing lawyer was downright nasty, but they did get a favorable settlement. "On the way out of the courthouse we passed the opposing attorney in the hall. The two of us wanted to run up to him and jeer, 'Nyah, nyah, nyah.' But Purcell [their lawyer] beat us to the punch. He said, 'See you around, Mike.' The other attorney smiled and said, 'OK, Bob, have a good weekend.' Afterward we asked Purcell how he had managed to keep cool. He gave us the long-suffering look one gives young innocents, which we were, and said simply, 'Oh, it's all part of the game.'"

Like that courtroom lawyer, you want to remember to keep your options open at home, and to forgive and forget when you and your partner have resolved the issue.

We have to remind ourselves constantly that our partner is first and foremost a person, a vulnerable person who doesn't want to lose face any more than we do, and who will react badly if he feels he is being unfairly attacked or manipulated. Think of the cost of having to be right; after all, knowing that you are the absolute authority on a subject or the one who carries the flame of justice does not necessarily mean you'll be happy. Whenever there is a clear winner, there are actually two losers. The winner can bask in her glory a bit too long and lose sight of what her partner is feeling; the loser can become resentful and sabotage the outcome, either sooner or later. In short, don't let a bargaining session mess up a relationship—either a professional or a personal one.

BE WILLING TO GIVE

As they say in the stock market, you can be a bear or a bull but you can't be a pig.

The deadliest way to sabotage a negotiation, and with it a relationship, is to push too hard to try to get something for nothing. Author Michael Korda describes how self-defeating win-lose negotiations are: "You can't negotiate anything by digging in your heels and refusing to budge. There has to be a certain willingness to give, if you're going to get what *you* want. For reasons that lie deep in the human psyche, people who can grasp this simple fact perfectly well in everyday life often ignore it in their intimate personal relationships."

When a dispute erupts in the privacy of our homes, we often fall into a familiar tug-of-war. "I want to buy a new sofa; you're too cheap," you say accusingly, as you try to pull him over the line. "I don't want new furniture; we don't have the money," he retorts and gives the rope a hard jerk, trying to drag you over to defeat. In the heat of the discussion, we can get caught up in the battle and concentrate on making him give in or suffer a loss rather than resolve what we are fighting about. Conflicts with coworkers are never pleasant, but when you have a conflict with your mate, sharp words have a particularly painful sting.

At work, when a tense situation arises between you and a coworker, "approach your colleague in a neutral, matter-of-fact way," prompts Robert Bramson, a management consultant and author of *Coping with Difficult People*. "Remember that your purpose is not to point a finger or defend your position in the office, but to find a solution to a situation that is clearly troubling both of you."

That is exactly the approach Anne, who is an artist by night and a legal secretary by day, used to deal with a tense situation on her job. Anne's coworker became increasingly hostile and resentful of Anne's taking vacation time to enter art shows. Because Anne strung out her vacation days to participate in as many shows as she could, the office atmosphere was becoming very uncomfortable and stressful.

In a situation like this one, "describe your own experience as specifically and nonjudgmentally as possible," advises Bramson. And that is what Anne did. She was direct and said, "When I take a vacation day to participate in an art show, I get the feeling you resent me for it and think I'm not doing my fair share of the work around here. Am I somewhere in the ballpark?"

Like Anne, after you have spoken your piece you must give the other person a chance to respond without interruption. Your colleague has to feel that you have a high regard for her feelings. "Bite your tongue if you have to; you need to hear her out completely to learn what she's upset about. Expect to get dumped on, but instead of saying anything in response, just nod to convey you understand her anger," recommends Bramson.

If a solution doesn't readily surface, don't reignite hostilities by counterattacking her. Instead, acknowledge her side of the story. "Say 'If that's how you see the situation, it must be frustrating,'" coaches Brian DesRoches, a Seattle-based therapist. "If you don't launch into a defensive counterattack as she might expect, it will make her stop for a moment and think about her own emotions and how they could be feeding into the conflict."

By listening carefully to her viewpoint, you tune in to understanding the real problem and are more able to discuss a solution. "I realized that my taking vacation days wasn't what really irritated her," related Anne. "What made her upset was that she felt left behind because I had an exciting 'second career.' She felt that she was stuck picking up the pieces in the office after me, and that I was not as committed to the job as she was. What became very clear to me was that the problem wasn't really work-related, but a difference in how we balanced work and personal time. I decided that the best move was to stop talking about my art projects in the office. Over the next few weeks, I reiterated that I enjoyed my job and could be counted on to pitch in. Paying attention to our office relationship and keeping a low profile about my art really turned things around. She stopped sniping at me and even wished me a 'good vacation' the last time I left for a few days."

When you and your partner are presented with a thorny disagreement, it's possible that the conflict springs from misunderstandings or a simple lack of communication. But sometimes we just aren't paying enough attention to how our actions are perceived by others. Tracy, a computer systems consultant, faced such a conflict with her husband, Ed, a contractor with the federal government. She dubbed the crisis "The Great Watering Project." In her words, "We live on five acres of land and have a good sized vegetable garden, plus a field of alfalfa. Because our climate is so dry we have to be vigilant about watering the fields. It is a real pain in the neck to keep up with it. The problem is not with who waters, it is with how we water. I move the hoses around from place to place as I think it is needed. He, on the other hand, uses a very precise system of rotating the hoses. Ed began to drop hostile remarks in my direction complaining that I wasn't holding up my fair share of the bargain. It made me very upset. Finally, I confronted him about his accusations very directly."

By applying the same fundamentals of win-win communication as Anne did with her coworker, Tracy cleared the air with Ed. She listened carefully to Ed's point of view without trying to justify herself. She listened for the *underlying* problem. And by listening, she learned that Ed, rightly or wrongly, felt she acted as if she had no regard for how important the garden was to him, and therefore didn't really value him.

Even though she felt Ed was off base, Tracy focused on how they could avoid future hurt feelings. Ed agreed to accept the reality that Tracy will never care as much about the task of watering as he does, and he consented to making the garden smaller and more manageable. Tracy vowed to try harder to use his system, and suggested that they plant some cutting flowers to make the garden more interesting to her. Tracy laughed when she told me how, after the next harvest, Ed acknowledged she did a good job for a "city girl."

The strategy that both Tracy and Anne used is what I call the willing-to-listen and willing-to-change school of conflict resolution. Pate Glacel, president of Pace Consulting Group, Inc., a management consulting firm, supports this gentle but action-oriented approach to dealing with sticky issues. On the job, Glacel believes that demonstrating your willingness to do what needs to be done is one of the most effective ways to defuse a colleague's resentment. It certainly is a way to defuse a lover's resentment. By avoiding harsh words and approaching the misunderstanding with a loving regard for her partner, Tracy opened up a dialogue instead of starting an argument. And that is the most important goal of all. The successful negotiation is one that leaves both of you feeling respected and valued by the other.

Your relationship with your mate is more important in the long run than the issue on the bargaining table. Remind yourself that, unlike war and Scrabble, the goal of partnership is to nourish goodwill and good feelings for each other, not to claim victory over your opponent.

PUT NEEDS BEFORE WANTS

Instead of arguing on the basis of wants, discuss what each person needs. When partners bargain over needs rather than wants, they are a lot more likely to find a solution that benefits them both. Separate the "must haves" from the "would like to haves." Are your nonnegotiables reasonable, or are they emotional and ego driven?

Christine, who administers a senior citizens' program, tells us how she dealt with a "must-have" situation by putting a humorous twist on a standard management negotiation technique.

94

"Jim and I have a wonderful relationship except for one major thing: downtime after work. I need to have some time all to myself to recharge my batteries when I get home from work. I don't want to talk; I don't want to 'relate.' I just want to be all by myself for twenty to thirty minutes. We agreed that he would not interrupt me or expect me to be available. But he could never do it. It was always something. Sometimes he couldn't find something. Or he would need to take just a minute of my time to inquire about dinner, or the mail, or the dog, whatever. When I called him on stepping on my solitude, he would shrug his shoulders and say, 'Not intended.' I felt he just wasn't sensitive to my needs at all. He would get his feelings hurt and feel that I was being selfish.

"I complained about all of this to a friend of mine who happens to be a director of human resources development. Her advice was to use the standard peer review/evaluation technique by setting up an appointment with Jim to review the standards, goals, and objectives of our job descriptions as spouses. I was a bit skeptical, but desperate, so I set an appointment with Jim and advised him we would be doing this review. I asked him to bring to our meeting a written evaluation of my wifely job performance. I decided to have a little fun with it—I put on my proper professional demeanor, placed a label with his name on it on a large brown envelope, typed up an agenda, and poured the wine. I dispassionately reviewed his performance as a spouse who respected his partner's need for solitude. (No bonus this year.) Then, he rated me. (Interpersonal relations—needs improvement.) It broke the ice, and we dealt with how we could better handle my need for time out and his feelings of being shut out. The solution? I would give him five or ten minutes of my undivided post-work attention, and he would leave me to my own devices for a half hour. What is really odd is that my need for downtime has nearly evaporated. Maybe I was just planting my feet in the ground to make a point?"

Christine's sense of humor allowed her to deal with conflict in a way that some people might not to be able to pull off so easily. Still, her approach clearly illustrates that just talking about your needs isn't enough. You must be prepared to state what you need in specific terms: why it is important to you (in this case, lack of solitude was negatively affecting Christine's marriage), and what you are willing to trade to get it. Once you have your trade-offs straight, you have to screw up your courage and go for it. Do it in your own way, but as the Nike advertisement shouts, "Just do it."

PICK AN OPTIMAL TIME

Professional negotiators recommend that once you've decided to enter into a bargaining dialogue, seek the most optimal time for the meeting. If you were hoping to launch a new project in the office and needed to negotiate to get the cooperation of someone else, you wouldn't just plant yourself in front of her desk. You would carefully check out the calendar for conflicting meetings, and you would select a time when you are at your best and the other person is most likely to be responsive.

On the job we prepare for our negotiations; we put the research together, prepare the case, and set up a tight argument for proceeding with the project. Then we put it on a calendar. The same careful preparation is the key to successful negotiating at home.

Don't expect your spouse to drop everything and pay attention just because he loves you and you want him to do so. If we come home stressed out from our workday or are just tired and cranky, we aren't likely to be positive or cooperative. Watch out for HALT conditions: being Hungry, Angry, Lonely, or Tired. Each of these conditions is widely believed to lead to conflict. Ask yourself, "Is this a good time to resolve this dispute?" If any one of the HALT conditions prevail for you or your partner, the answer is no.

Francis Roe offers this suggestion: "The best time to start any kind of domestic negotiations is after a really delicious meal. (It's desirable but not essential to prepare it yourself.) Give him an extra glass or two of zinfandel, but tonight you stick to Perrier."

To bring up an issue at a bad time is a setup for disappointment and frustration—it feeds into feeling rejected. If your partner feels strung out and rejects your overture for a problem-solving session, don't take his grumpiness personally. Just find a better time to have a serious discussion. Realize that when we are stressed, it may take all of the social graces we can muster to be even politely inattentive to someone who wants our attention. That's just the way people react to exhaustion or stress, and that goes for our coworkers, our boss, ourselves and, of course, our spouse.

PUT YOURSELF IN HIS POSITION

"Try to figure out the other person's response in advance," advises stockbroker Mary Beth Sullivan. "What is your boss likely to say when you ask for a raise? How will your client react when you announce you've increased your fees?" In other words, try to imagine what your negotiations will look like and how you will handle the trade-offs. It's essentially the same tactic at home.

Suppose your partner seems reluctant to attend a social function with you. You enjoy such events and want (need) the outlet they provide, but feel uncomfortable going without him. How do you negotiate this? First, you analyze the situation to determine why he doesn't want to go. It may have nothing to do with you, the party, or the people who would be there. Perhaps he is feeling tired from work and needs to spend time alone. If that's the case, offer to trade a camping or other getaway weekend for a social weekend sometime later when he is more into socializing. By identifying what he really wants and proposing a way you can fulfill that need, you can negotiate from a position of power—you have something to trade. And the more things you can trade, the stronger your bargaining position will be. "When you're negotiating," advises Francis Roe, "always have a small bag of giveaway goodies, items you don't truly care about but that can be used as bargaining chips. Giving him the first goody for nothing can do a lot to establish your goodwill." Louise, a professor of history, agrees. She believes, "You should decide what is important to you and what isn't. When Russ and I bought a new car last year he got to pick out the color because it was important to him and not to me. I bargained for selecting the sound system."

Claudia, who directs a large sales force for a medical supply office, employs a technique she calls "bargaining and strategy planning." This includes the effective principles of making a sale, bargaining to achieve a positive outcome, and closing a deal. Some of you will no doubt protest. Use sales techniques on our partner? Too manipulative. Too phoney. But keep an open mind, and heed Claudia's comments: "Women do tend to see sales techniques as a form of manipulation. When they first come aboard they usually say, 'I don't want to manipulate anyone to make a sale.' Men have a different appreciation for sales. They see getting someone to do what you want them to do as 'bargaining and strategy planning.'

"In making a sale, you have to accept the basic premise that some people have a hard time coming out and turning you down; therefore they will usually not be direct in rejecting your offer. Some people do say 'no' and mean it, and it's very clear that you won't be making a sale to them that day, or maybe ever. Other people may want to purchase the product but something is making them feel ambivalent or hesitant. A good salesperson helps the person clarify their objections, offers alternatives, and steers the customer into making an affirmative decision. The goal is to turn the 'no' or 'maybe' into a 'yes.'

"It took me years to figure out that I could be applying what I know about making a deal to getting my goals met at home. Alan and I have strong preferences, and we would get into stalemates over simple things like eating out. I love to eat out and he doesn't. Unfortunately, both of us are lousy cooks. Typically, I would ask him, 'Do you want to go out for Chinese food?' And nine times out of ten—he has no trouble with being direct—John would reply, 'No.' I would pout and hope he would come around and acquiesce just to put a smile on my face. This little saga was played out more times than I care to admit. (Food isn't our only difference, but it is a good example.) One night he told me that if I wanted to go out to eat, I should just go. It was a shock; I realized that wasn't the deal I wanted to make. I wanted to be with him *and* go out to a restaurant. After I got over my bruised feelings, I recognized that I had been using the wrong approach, known as beating around the bush.

"The fundamental principle of sales is to be direct and make it clear what it is that you want to see happen. I had expected Alan to read my mind and fulfill my wishes even though I hadn't spoken my preference. Now I'm direct. 'I would like to go out for Chinese food. Would you like to go?' If he says no, but I really have a strong preference for food I don't have to cook, I apply a different sales technique—clarifying the objection. If a client says they can't afford to buy right now, I ask if it would work for them if we put it on a payment plan. Or if I could defer payment for sixty days, would they be able to manage it? I *consult* with the client to clear away the barriers in their way. Applying this to my negotiations with Alan, I offer him alternatives: Would he prefer to go out for something other than Chinese? Or would it work better for him if we went later on in the evening? Or should we order take-out and have it delivered? I've since learned that he wasn't objecting so much to compromising, but to handing over the decision making to him and not taking responsibility for owning up to what I wanted. It was ridiculous that for years I believed it was too contrived to apply my interpersonal skills to the most important personal relationship I have. I wonder what techniques Alan is using on me? Whatever, something is working because we are very happy."

A critical factor in this success story is that Claudia, by putting herself in Alan's shoes, was able to see their differences with a fresh eye. She focused on how she affected Alan instead of focusing on his effect on her. Then she applied to her marriage her decision-making skills, her knowledge of applied psychology, and a keen sense of what will work and what won't. To make your negotiations as effective as Claudia's, you have to take her approach. Think about your own personality and that of your mate, then strategically use your ability to make deals to bargain for a compatible way to live with your differences.

BE RESOURCEFUL IN FINDING SOLUTIONS

Last month my car went belly up and had to be towed to a garage. I had to be at the airport in two hours to pick up an important client. What to do? Simple. I'd use my spouse's car. But when I called him, he informed me that he needed his car. We began to debate whose need was more urgent. Listening in (there was no way to ignore my end of the conversation), the woman at the desk of the auto repair shop shyly whispered a suggestion. "Why don't you rent a car?" Well, that was a thought. I halted my argument in mid-sentence and in no time buzzed off to the airport in my nice little rental car. Why hadn't I seen how easy it was to resolve the issue? Because when you get stuck in the groove of a problem, it's difficult to see beyond it.

If in the middle of a crisis or a dispute you find yourself running dry about how to resolve the problem, don't dig deeper into the same well. Use the technique of brainstorming to help you think more creatively about how to come to a resolution.

What should you do, for example, if a coworker complains about having to fill in for you when you're away from your desk? "Sit down and think it through with the other person," recommends Darlene Orlov, president of Orlov Resources for Business, a consulting firm in New York City. Acknowledge that you can't solve the problem alone. You might say, as Orlov directs, "It does happen that emergency calls sometimes come from clients after I've left. I agree it's not right for other people to have to deal with my calls when I'm not here. Let's figure out a better way to handle the situation."

Many people find it difficult to be resourceful in their personal relationship because they've fallen into the habit of arguing. To climb out of the groove, it helps to join forces with your partner and get creative. First, reject all old solutions you have tried before. Then let anything that pops into your head come out. Get a little crazy. Think up all kinds of ways to resolve the problem—wild, impractical ways. Eventually, a practical solution will emerge, and you can move on. Psychologist Barbara Brown recommends, "Each person needs to be responsible for creative solutions that meet both their own and their partners' needs. Use solutions as tentative experiments. See what works. Go back to the drawing board together if one plan fails. Become good researchers about each other's desires."

The moral: When you hit a wall, climb over it, go around it, or dig a tunnel under it.

IMPLICIT BARGAINING

Besides the obvious strategies we use to bargain with our mate, there is another important but less visible way that we deal with each other: implicit bargaining. Bargaining isn't always conscious. Often we are not in the least aware that we are engaged in trading off something for something else. For instance, at the office we might give high praise to a subordinate for a job well done and offer to make sure his superior effort is noted in his personnel file. Thus a subtle bargain is struck for future reference: you give support and positive reinforcement, and in return you receive (or we hope you receive) a happy employee who's forever in your debt and a job well done that makes your department look good. Without being explicit ("I'll trade you two 'attaboys' for each excellent report!"), an unspoken pact exists between the two of you.

Many of the bargains struck at home with your spouse are apt to be just as subtle. Of course, explicit bargains—those that you're conscious of making—are easy to identify. It's the implicit trades that are less clear-cut. If you think about what's happening, though, you may realize that implicit trade-offs occur frequently when you interact with your mate. A simple example: your mate, like your subordinate at the office, responds positively to praise (who doesn't?) and negatively to nagging and reproach. When something goes wrong and you give him loving support instead of a lecture, you can expect him to provide the same safety net for you when you need it. It's a bargaining process—intangible, but real nevertheless.

Analyze some of your typical trade-offs a little further, and you'll understand what sort of commodities you and your spouse have implicitly placed on the bargaining table. Trading off watching television shows, going for a walk instead of playing cards, sex in the morning instead of the evening. These are likely to be of far more influence in a relationship than the deals that are verbalized. But be a little cautious about always taking these unspoken bargains for granted or making assumptions based on them. An implicit bargain can cause considerable trouble when the other person isn't aware he made a deal and that we are expecting a trade-off. It's a sure way to be disappointed and angry when our unsuspecting partner doesn't come through.

Yet on the whole, those unspoken bargains are what makes our relationship hum along so contentedly. Think of how well you and your spouse do handle the give-and-take of living with each other. When you are unhappy about something in your relationship it helps to remember the pleasant way you handle so many kinds of everyday trade-offs. In other words, keep the dispute in context. As my friend Kay Scott reminds me, "Make molehills out of molehills."

FIRST AND LAST: COMMUNICATE

Whether we are engaged in spoken or unspoken bargains, our success in negotiating with our mate is dependent upon how well we communicate with each other. Not surprisingly, the overall quality of our relationship is linked to our ability to communicate.

In a detailed study of communication between married couples, J. M. Gottman, author of *Marital Interaction,* found a number of differences between what he labeled "distressed" and "nondistressed" relationships. He wrote that "distressed" couples are more apt to express feelings by employing such tactics as sarcasm and ridicule. They tend to try to "read" each other's feelings and often interpret those feelings as negative, even when their partner is not speaking negatively. Distressed couples also establish a rigid, broken-record pattern of communication while nondistressed partners use a variety of ways to communicate in their conversations.

Unhappy couples perpetuate their conflicts through "negative, often punishing, verbal exchanges that may just keep getting worse the longer a couple continues to talk." Ironically, even when both partners want to share their feelings with each other and are very keen on finding better ways of negotiating each other's needs and wants, they don't connect.

It's frustrating, but not unusual. Deborah Tannen, in her bestselling book *You Just Don't Understand: Women and Men in Conversation,* states that there is an "epidemic of failed conversation among wives and husbands." In her research she found that "most wives want husbands to be, first and foremost, conversational partners, but few husbands share this expectation of their wives."

When you think about it, it is a marvel that men and women can communicate at all. From the time we are wee tots men and women develop different styles of communication and use language for completely different purposes. Girls use communication to seek validation and intimacy. This involves developing language that helps build supportive relationships and closeness within small groups. Boys use language to maintain and demonstrate their independence and to negotiate for power and status, rather than to achieve mutual support.

Besides the disparity in our conversational goals, we also differ in the language we use. And those differences provide a ripe opportunity for miscues and misunderstanding, the two factors that most quickly kill negotiations.

WOMENSPEAK/MENSPEAK

> When a door is open and a draft is coming through, men will say, "Please close the door." Women more often say, "It's cold in here."
>
> —Leslie Linthicum, journalist

The differences in male and female speech show up early. Deborah Tannen describes listening to separate groups of second-grade girls and boys talk. "I had the feeling," she writes, "I was looking at two different species."

In my seminars, when I observe the now grown-up boys and girls trying to communicate as men and women, I often see them handicapped by the lack of a common language. It's not that men and women don't communicate; certainly we talk and listen to each other. But that doesn't mean we are getting through. "I think it's more of a problem when people think they are speaking the same language," declares Jean Newman, chairwoman of the Linguistics Department at the University of New Mexico. "They seem to be speaking your language but they're really not. The differences are more subtle, and that's why they lead to problems."

"Conversation may be a snare that disguises how badly we're communicating," explains Francis Roe. "Like the Britisher who thought that communication with Americans would be easy because they spoke the same language. Pay attention to semantics. His words don't always mean the same thing as yours." Leslie Linthicum, a staff writer for *The Albuquerque Journal,* agrees and points out that, "Because men and women are able to communicate with some ease, frequently they are unaware of their different styles, which can lead to problems. If women in management positions ask for information indirectly, they can be labeled ineffective. Men who suggest solutions to their girlfriends' problems instead of sympathizing may be labeled uncaring."

These unique differences between menspeak and womenspeak are hardly news. In recent years there have been countless articles and books on the disparity in conversational styles of men and women. And that information is helpful. We can't improve communication until we are aware of the differences, or possible differences, between our partners and ourselves. So what exactly are these differences?

Generally, women tend to be more responsive then men in conversation. We tend to interject words of encouragement when listening to someone speak. I read once that the Japanese have a word, *aizuchi,* for this listener-talk. It means a constant stream of response. A lot of uh-huh, uh-huh, hmmm, yes, oh yeah. The glitch is that men regard our encouraging sounds and words as signs of consensus, while women use aizuchi to show we are actively listening and following the conversation. When the woman then disagrees or offers another viewpoint, the man may feel misled or think she is, as men told me, being two-faced.

Likewise, women think men aren't listening when there is an absence of verbal and physical listening signals, while men think their silence conveys their full attention. (My theory is that men are born with an Instant Verbal Replay Feature. Actually, I have proof. When I'm talking to my partner and he appears to be going into a deep trance, the IVRF automatically goes into "record" mode. In midsentence I've stopped and accused him of tuning me out—"You're not listening!" He gets a crafty male "I gotcha" look in his eyes as the IVRF kicks into play, and he then repeats everything I've said, *verbatim*. (Really, how do men pull that off?)

Women want to talk about and resolve whatever is going amiss in the relationship. But men sometimes interpret their partner's need to talk about what is bothering her as a potential personal attack. "A man just wants to solve a problem and be done with it," says Judith Sills, Ph.D., a Philadelphia clinical psychologist. "A woman will hash and rehash the same point for hours. Basically, men want to head straight for a resolution, and women are more interested in the process of resolving." Men usually try to postpone or end the conflict while contributing less to the conflict-resolution process than women. This is because, as Denver University psychologist Howard Markman observes, "Compared to women, men seem to have substantial difficulty handling negative emotions and conflict."

Because women pay such close attention to their partner, they are better at predicting what their mate will say; they reciprocate their partner's emotional tone more often. They also tend to be more aware of what is going on emotionally in their relationship. They sense trouble brewing before their partner does, and they keep tabs on the relationship with some regularity, while their spouse only thinks about it if there seems to be a problem.

A woman's tendency to include details that create intimacy is one reason that men think women talk too much. And a man's tendency to share his knowledge—invited or not—makes women think that all men do is lecture.

As a general rule, men feel more entitled to have their own way, so they tend to be straightforward about asserting themselves. They are more likely to use direct approaches, such as asking, telling, and reasoning to get what they want. And if that doesn't work, men will resort to the next level: intimidation or digging their heels in until they wear their adversary down. Although men's pragmatism is something to be admired, their dogged insistence on getting their own way isn't such a winsome trait. Unfortunately, all too often it intimidates us and we back down.

A woman wants an empathetic listener and a man thinks she will never get to the point. Men talking to other men get used to fast-paced conversations that typically stay on the surface with respect to emotions; that enable them to get practical tips or offer advice to others; and that are usually pragmatic. Women are used to conversations that, while practical, are also a major source of emotional support, self-understanding, and the understanding of others.

The difference in our styles can produce friction. A woman is likely to be surprised and angered by a man's need to immediately solve an issue she brings up in the conversation. Adding to her anger, contend psychologists Mark Sherman and Adelaide Haas, may be her belief that "men don't credit her with good sense and intelligence, and that perhaps that is why he is advising her. The fact is, he does the same with male friends."

Jane Campbell, a contributing writer for the *Utne Reader*, helps us see that particular male trait in a lighter vein. "Men always have opinions, even on subjects they know nothing about," Campbell declares. She describes this male compulsion to answer questions regardless of actual knowledge as the "Male Answer Syndrome." While this male need to provide women with answers annoys us, it has redeeming qualities. Campbell notes, "Sometimes this expansiveness is appealing. If you ask a woman, 'Why does Mary Hart wear those sweaters?' she will shrug helplessly, acknowledging that some things are simply unknowable. A man, on the other hand, will come up with a few theories (She's related to the designer? Color-blind?). Men have the courage and the inventiveness to try to explain the inexplicable."

Admittedly, each individual and each couple is unique, and these stereotypical gender communication problems may not apply to your situation at all. Naturally there are men who are good listeners and women who routinely give direct advice. Still, it is helpful to recognize our differences, if any, and respect them. When our negotiations with our spouse appear to be going the way of two ships passing in the night, we can stop and question whether or not the problem is one of male versus female communication styles. If you detect you aren't connecting, stop and adjust your style to be more effective.

For example:

- Get to the point quickly. If you try to ease him into the conversation, you'll lose him. Summarize first. Fill in the plot later.

- Relinquish the interesting slice-of-life details (she had on a pink fuzzy angora blend sweater from the . . .). Take a page from a Hemingway novel—keep it crisp, lean, sparse.

- If you share a problem with your mate, let him know what you need and expect. If you don't want his advice, say so.

- Don't psychoanalyze your mate. ("You always need to be the center of attention because your mother didn't go to your Little League baseball games.")

- Be specific, avoid generalizations.

- Stick to the issues and stand your ground even if he resorts to a little bullying. However, if he gets mean spirited, withdraw quickly and firmly.

- Don't apologize for needing to talk. I'm sure this is one of the basic rights granted by the constitution to all females.

It is helpful to apply the knowledge we have about the differences between his and her negotiating methods to improve our communications with men, on and off the job. But there is a special urgency for women to be aware of "womenspeak." It is a spoiler in all we do to create equality between ourselves and our partners.

THE PENALTY FOR GIRL TALK

Alfie Kohn, a contributing editor to *Psychology Today,* compiled the research of Robin Lakoff of the University of California, Berkeley, and Pamela Fishman of the University of California, Santa Barbara, to discover that "questioning is a distinctive characteristic of women's speech." Since questioning is such a female trait, ask yourself as I review the findings of this research, "Does this sound like me? If so, is it effective? If not, how can I change it?"

Khon's findings can briefly be summed up as follows:

- *Women ask more questions.* In fact, women tend to ask three times as many questions as men in mixed-gender groups. Not bad in itself, but be aware of the danger of appearing as if you are on a date trying to get a shy guy to talk.
- *Women make statements in a questioning tone.* ("I saw an, um, interesting report from the home office today(?).") The rising inflection sounds as if it were a question. It suggests that the speaker needs affirmation even though she may be the only one who has the necessary information or is the one who has an opinion to offer. It is annoying.
- *Women use more tag questions.* Adding a brief question at the end of a sentence (". . . don't you think so?") signals doubt or gives the listener the message that the speaker needs reassurance rather than agreement. Not all of the studies concluded that women use more tag questions than men.
- *Women tend to lead off with questions.* Starting a conversation with a short question ("You know what?") is intended to get the listener's attention while inviting him to get involved. It usually isn't effective because it has an off-putting side to it: it sounds mindless.

- *Women use more hedges, or qualifiers ("kinda," "sorta"), and rely on intensifiers ("really").* In the latter case, the speaker often does more than use a word; the emphasis with which it is pronounced ("wooonderfulll") tells the listener how to react. Most listeners (count me as one) find it irritating or phoney.
- *Women—particularly young women—use "like" English more often than do men.* This is my contribution to the research of Lakoff and Fishman. I can't prove it scientifically, but I speak with thousands of men and women every year and I hear many more female voices using "like" as an adjective. "It was, like, a movie." "He was, like, a nice guy." The problem is that it sounds, um, like a California Valley Girl(?). Unfortunately, females who speak this way have a reputation among the rest of the population for not exactly being rocket scientists. Valley speak isn't limited to California girls—I've heard it all over the country. If you are guilty of this linguistic folly, it would be well worth your while to break yourself of the habit.

Over the last decade we have become more aware of the implications of the above findings. Women's traditionally submissive, tentative speech patterns are a disadvantage to them in a can-do and speak-out business culture. It works against us at home, too. Most men, given their assertive negotiating postures, have the edge in getting what they want out in the business world or at home.

I don't want to give the impression that I think women are at fault or are spineless Barbie Dolls when we communicate in women-speak. We women are in a double bind. As Lakoff notes, a woman is "ostracized as unfeminine by both men and women" if she is straightforward and assertive, but dismissed as "someone not to be taken seriously, of dim intelligence, frivolous," if she falls back on a traditional feminine style in her speech patterns.

WHAT CAN A WOMAN SAY?

We have to untangle ourselves from our womenspeak legacy. "Make suggestions in declarative sentences, not framed as questions," advises Pat Heim in *Hardball for Women,* a book that is required reading for all women (men benefit as well). She offers the following power-talk strategies:

- Take as much time as you need and speak assertively, with low pitch.
- Don't wait for others to invite you to speak before you join in.
- If interrupted, ignore the interrupter and keep on talking, but be careful to avoid stridency.
- Don't turn statements into questions, especially if you are under fire.
- Avoid tag questions, and swing that voice down at the end of your statement.
- Avoid hedging in presenting your ideas; make positive assertions.
- Banish the verb *try* from your vocabulary.
- Don't discount what you're saying before you even say it. Let your listeners draw their own conclusions.

Although traditional women's language has some very big disadvantages in terms of communicating powerfully, many linguists believe it also has features that are worth keeping. Being considerate of how you ask for something, paying attention to the other person's need to talk, and listening more actively and effectively are valuable social skills.

Linguist Sally McConnell-Ginet of Cornell University urges women to "adopt a conversational style that doesn't sacrifice sensitivity but nevertheless doesn't make you sound as if you have less commitment to your beliefs than you have." It is encouraging that many more of us in business are overcoming powerless speech patterns in order to succeed in our careers. We have had to, in order to gain respect, express our views (and have them listened to), and negotiate with colleagues and clients to get what we want. Women's tendency to express their thoughts masked in womenspeak will eventually fade. As women occupy more powerful positions in our society there will be less need for them to use the wiles of powerless language to be accepted socially or professionally.

This brings us to the last frontier of finding our own vibrant, assertive voice: the home front. It's difficult not to fall back into those sweetie-pie, ultrafeminine speech patterns when we are sitting across the bargaining table from the man we love. For one thing, it's the way women have always manipulated men to get what they wanted from them. For another, men eat it up, so it's a tough habit to break. But if we want to be treated like a competent woman we have to put those girlish ploys aside. To negotiate for what we need and want in our intimate partnership, we must speak with confidence and with the expectation of being taken seriously—as we are learning to do in our work.

Keep in mind the following advice.

> Remember the dignity of your womanhood.
> Do not appeal. Do not beg. Do not grovel.
> Take courage.
> —Christabel Pankhurst, British suffragette

In the pages ahead, we'll turn our attention to other hurdles that often impede our journey toward partnership—specifically, the entrenched sex role expectations surrounding the power of money, and the ways men and women divvy up the housework. We'll look at how you can apply the negotiating techniques we've revealed here to overcome the conflict over money and household tasks in your personal life.

5

DEALING WITH THE REALITY OF UNEQUAL PAYCHECKS

We tell ourselves that money makes no difference to lovers. Passion, power, and paychecks are unrelated, we say, but clearly that's a fantasy. In reality, even though the romantic in us denies it, money—who has it, who doesn't—is a major player in our relationships. "Most people like to think that the right to affect decisions is based on the demands of daily events, on which partner is wiser on a certain issue, or on special gifts of persuasion," observe Philip Blumstein and Pepper Schwartz, the authors of *American Couples.* "They do not like to think that income, something that comes into the relationship from the outside, imposes a hierarchy on the couple. But it does. In three out of four types of couples we studied, we find that the amount of money a person earns—in comparison with a partner's income—establishes relative power."

The cold truth is that love can take a beating from money; our partnership doesn't exist beyond the realm of ordinary economic concerns. Along with our take-home pay we take home attitudes as well, and most women's goal of equal partner-ship is sabotaged by unequal paychecks.

Ideally, money in and of itself would not automatically give one partner power over the other. But it does. Money and power are directly related, no matter how far we've come toward achieving equality with the man in our life. Although women may persistently try to brush aside or gloss over the way finances dictate marital power, the truth won't go away simply because we find it unseemly, unfeminine, or threatening. Money issues are important and difficult ones for a couple seeking to be equal in all things.

There are no easy answers, but there are steps we can take to minimize the damage of women's and men's lopsided earnings. As a guide, we can study the experiences of women who have dealt effec-tively with the issue of power and finances in their partnerships. Then we can explore some ways for women to break the pattern of "moneyphobia"—a vicious cycle of fear and confusion that prevents us from effectively earning, negotiating, investing, and managing our incomes. Finally, we have the advice of financial planners to help us take control of and balance our accounts.

THE GOLDEN RULE REVISED

In a perfect world, women would be able to split the rent and the restaurant check, but in real life most of us can't afford to share and share alike with our men. True, we *are* better off in the work force than we were years ago. The success stories of women leap off the pages of dozens of magazines and newspapers. But for most of us, the gender gap between women's and men's earnings hasn't narrowed perceptibly. Most women, even those working full-time, are at the disadvantage of earning less money than their spouses. Wives still earn only about 70–75 percent of their husband's income. In fact, women's earnings have hovered between 60 and 70 percent of men's for more than *forty* years; in the mid-fifties, women who worked full-time earned 64 percent of what men earned. Today only one in six working women brings home more money than her spouse, and this figure has remained constant for a decade.

If you accept the theory that the resources each person brings to a relationship largely shape his or her relative bargaining power, it is easy to see why most working wives wield less power than their husbands. Though working women in general have more to bargain with than do nonemployed wives, they still have considerably fewer chips in the power game than their husbands. The bottom line? He who has the gold, rules.

A woman's lesser-of-two-equals status isn't always obvious at first glance. For example, in many couples the woman deposits the checks, pays the bills, doles out the lunch money, and keep tabs on the daily accounting. In fact, an overwhelming 82 percent of the women replying to Shere Hite's study, *Women in Love,* reported that they are in charge of the family funds. This includes even those whose husbands are the sole wage earners. But most women's money power is a mirage. Even among couples who view themselves as equals, the husband typically has the final say on big decisions because he earns the big money and thereby has the clout. Financial planner Michael Stein explains it this way: "While the wives might be more likely to manage day-to-day family finances like balancing the checkbook and paying household bills, the husbands usually have the upper hand in making the major financial decisions."

Do wives who earn more money than their spouses wear the mantle and inherit the traditional power that comes with being the breadwinner? We'll cover this issue in chapter six, but as a preview, the evidence is that wives with higher incomes gain greater financial autonomy. The higher a wife's income, the freer she is to spend money as she sees fit, and the less accountable she feels she has to be for how she allocates her own spending money. But in answer to the power question: no, she doesn't wield any more power than women who earn less than their spouses. Never underestimate the long arm of sex-role stereotyping and the established power roles assigned to us by society.

COMPENSATING FOR THE WAGE GAP

How many times have you found yourself compensating for a leaner paycheck by taking on a heftier chunk of the housework? Do you sometimes get the feeling that he resents your demands for equality because you can't contribute equally to the joint checking account? Is it difficult to stand up for your rights because you know that your life-style is mostly subsidized by him?

It may seem ridiculous for a woman in love to worry about not earning as much money as her spouse. For some women this would not only seem like a non-problem, it would seem like the pot of gold at the end of the rainbow or something they took for granted. After all, for centuries "marrying up" was the acknowledged goal of many a sweet young thing and certainly a goal parents had for their daughters. In fact, it is still the goal of women (and parents) in certain circles of society. But most of us feel very uncomfortable trying to balance our commitment to equal partnership against the money that tips the scale in our spouse's favor. If he earns a great deal more than we do, we may feel we owe him some kind of reimbursement, some compensation for our inability to split expenses down the middle.

Janet's case is a good example. She holds down a high-powered job, but she also spends an inordinate amount of her time at home functioning as secretary-domestic for her husband, whose income happens to be three times her own. Janet claims she does it not only to kick in her share but also to prove she isn't taking advantage of him. "I can't talk myself out of feeling that I have to pay him back somehow," she told me. "So I take on all sorts of responsibility I have neither the time nor the inclination to cope with, even though he doesn't expect me to do so. And I perform all sorts of small tasks for him that I might not do otherwise, like keeping track of the phone calls he hasn't returned yet."

Sure, it *shouldn't* make any difference that he makes so much more money; it's an advantage to you both, like a trump card. But before you know it, the computations can get overwhelmingly complicated. His money, your money, our money, his money. Because there is no way to reach economic parity with their partners, women like Janet struggle to define the terms of being an equal in their partnership. One major problem is that the amount she can afford to pay for, or pay half of, is usually inadequate to cover the standard of living he enjoys—and he doesn't want to downsize to her economic level of life-style.

Deloris, a sales representative for a manufacturing firm, tells me that the first year she lived with Vince she found herself doing the same thing as Janet. "I felt as if I had to make up for not having as much money as he did—taking the clothes to the dry cleaners, picking up after him, and all of that little wifey stuff. In my business it's either feast or famine; I don't have a steady flow of money. We pool our money, but when it was famine and I had no income to contribute, I felt like a kept woman. It was beginning to be a big problem to me. We talked about it but he didn't understand why I was so unhappy about the situation. He'd say, 'It's our money.'

"But I worked out a way to deal with the issue that helps me keep my self-esteem. One day at the office, I took a client to lunch and had to use the petty cash fund. I realized I could use this same cash-flow system to manage money at home. At least for now. We started a discretionary account, treating it like a petty cash fund in that we don't have to be accountable for how we spend the money. When I get paid I put 10 percent of what I earn into it, and so does he. Either one of us can use it as we see fit. He does put more money in than I do, but I've had to resign myself to the fact that he earns more money so it's all right!"

Deloris is a realist. She can't do much more than she is doing to close the paycheck gap, so she does what she can to live with it by setting up a system that helps her maintain a sense of self-sufficiency. Often the biggest problem a woman faces over the lopsidedness of what he earns compared to what she earns has more to do with how to preserve her self-esteem than with dollars and dimes.

For some women, the issue revolves around independence. Being married and sharing decisions after years of being single and making decisions independently brings up a whole new set of issues to deal with. Take the case of Nancy, a high school principal, who told me, "Over the first year Tom and I were married, I fell into the habit of asking him what he thought of everything I wanted to buy. Not exactly for his approval; more to establish that he didn't disapprove. I'd been independent for years, and suddenly I was back in the role of a little girl asking her daddy for permission to spend her allowance. We put all of our money together—he earns a little more than I—but he didn't expect me to check out every purchase I made with him. Somehow I thought it was the right 'married' thing to do. I finally had to come to grips with how unhappy I was feeling. At the office, I'm in charge of my school's budget. I wouldn't think of asking the district supervisor to okay everything I buy. It is ridiculous that I gave up my authority to make my own financial decisions at home. Tom and I redid our budget so that we each have flexibility for things not on a fixed payment—such as clothes. I prefer to have the responsibility for using my own judgment about how my money is spent."

The choice doesn't have to be independence or no independence about money. As Nancy's experience proves, women's self-reliance and ability to manage their own money doesn't have to evaporate when they merge their lives with a man.

BALANCING THE BOOKS

It's going to be years before the economic playing field is leveled. Therefore, going out and earning a lot more money is not a realistic option for most women—at least not for now. To balance the books, we can become a financial partner in other ways. The most practical action we can take is to negotiate ways to divide up the responsibility for sharing expenses and managing money. The most important element in successfully working out the money issue is for both partners to participate equally in that decision-making process. It helps to know that many men dislike handling money. Don't assume that your partner has enjoyed being the one responsible for the finances. I have found that men often just take on this task because it is expected of them, whether they like it or not.

Remember, money is not just about money. It's a symbol of power, security, and who we are. For many men it's a measure of their manhood, their place in the pecking order. Some women who wouldn't wear anything but silk blouses clip coupons to save money on paper towels because they have a deep-seated fear of ending up as bag ladies. The most important thing to realize about money is that the need to control it may outweigh any measure of fiscal good sense. Couples argue more about how money is managed than about how much they have—and this holds true regardless of their actual income level.

It may be tedious for couples to create budgets together and decide jointly who will be responsible for what, but the effort is worth it. Consider the conclusion of the *American Couples* study: "When couples do take the time to share control over money management, they seem to have happier, calmer relationships." If the couple should suffer an economic setback, the previous planning and sharing of responsibility reduces harsh feelings and recriminations. They are more able to pull together as a team and go forward to solve the problem.

There are no hard-and-fast rules for accomplishing an equal economic partnership. There is no perfect composite picture that will fit every couple's needs. Nevertheless, there is one thing all couples face: whether or not they pool their money, it really isn't possible for the two partners to do all their spending separately and not in some ways impinge on each other's decisions ("You bought a *green* recliner to put on our blue rug?"). So they have to work out a system that both can live with.

The women I interviewed deal with money management in a number of different ways. Here's a sampling of their comments about four specific management techniques:

COUPLES SWITCH CONTROL EVERY OTHER YEAR

"We take turns being totally responsible for the bills and saving money every couple of years. It works out a lot better than when we were trying to split the responsibility."

"We discuss our financial plans but we take turns managing our finances. One year I'm responsible for bill-paying and savings, and the next year he is. We keep tally sheets and meet every month so that the person not in charge of the books keeps informed."

"When we managed our money together, we were always late in paying our bills. Taking turns for being the one in charge means that when it's your turn you know you have to get things done on time. There is nobody to blame but yourself."

EACH PERSON IS RESPONSIBLE FOR PAYING CERTAIN ITEMS EVERY MONTH

"My husband pays for rent and maintaining our vehicles. I pay for groceries and things like that. Whatever is left over from each of our checks is our spending money."

"I pay all my own expenses, and he does likewise. We generally split fifty-fifty on household items. We take turns paying for vacations and extra things."

"We have one joint savings account from which to pay one-time bills and the mortgage on the house and insurance. We take turns buying groceries. We pay for our own expenses such as medical bills and clothes."

ALL MONEY IS PUT INTO ONE ACCOUNT. CONTROL OF THE MONEY IS JOINT AND ONE PERSON MAY WRITE THE CHECKS FOR BILLS. BUT BOTH HAVE ACCESS TO THE MONEY AND INPUT INTO DECISIONS ABOUT HOW THE MONEY IS SPENT

"Our money goes into one pot, but I manage the money. I like financial arrangements. I am better at doing those things than he is, so I do it. We split the money after all the bills are paid."

THE COUPLE SPLITS EXPENSES FIFTY-FIFTY, USUALLY WITH SEPARATE BANK ACCOUNTS

"We have separate accounts. We like it this way. It solves a lot of conflicts. It works much better and I feel the independence to spend my money as I please."

"The only way it works for us is to keep our money separate. We put all of the bills in a pile and go over the budget together. We each pay half or one pays the whole thing and the other writes them a check for half. We put a percentage of our earnings aside for fun and that's our joint account."

Norma, a nurse practitioner I met in El Paso, Texas, had shared with me the latter strategy and then went on to describe their joint account. "We have a 'cash pot' to which we each contribute for entertainment and things we do together so we don't have to divide up checks or tickets fifty-fifty every time we go play. We keep the money in an old drawstring leather bag. Last year we decided to go see a movie at the very last minute. When we got to the theater Bruce leaped out and grabbed the bag to pay for the tickets. When we got to the ticket taker, she leaned over close to him and in a stage whisper said, 'Honey, didn't your Momma tell you that your purse should match your shoes?'"

Financial managers recommend that you know the advantages and disadvantages of the different approaches to managing money. For instance, one of the reasons for keeping separate accounts is "just in case . . ." It's not a pretty picture, but in this age of divorce many women feel the need to keep their assets separate. With joint accounts, by contrast, there is the risk that a departing partner can withdraw all the funds or, as one of my friends put it, "empty the pot on their way out." It takes real trust to joint account your assets. Another disadvantage is that with one checkbook and two check writers, the account can get scrambled if either forgets to record their checks. Most planners recommend three checking accounts—a joint household account for convenience, plus individual accounts to give each partner financial independence.

Caveat: It's only possible to set money management strategies in motion if you and your partner can deal with the finances calmly and rationally. Some men use their higher earnings as a way to dominate their spouse ("Who pays the bills around here?"). Some have the attitude that women can *earn* money but only men can cope with *managing* money. It is a slow and difficult process to initiate the changes needed to balance the partnership. Dr. Harriet B. Braiker advises, "It's important for a woman trying to deal with this kind of man to understand how deeply rooted these feelings can be so that she doesn't think these problems are her fault—or blame him unduly for emotions rooted in experiences that occurred long before she came into his life." As a couple, you may need to seek counseling if he isn't amenable to negotiating a more balanced system.

For the most part, we can believe in the possibility of change. Today's working women are using a lot of creativity to defuse some of the "power" in their mate's earning power. And, in general, men are grateful to be relieved of having to shoulder all of the burden as keeper of the couple's finances.

But there is still a remaining obstacle in the path to fiscal equality in marriage. Not only do we tend to *earn* less money than our mates, we *know* less about money. We manage money the old fashioned way: we ignore it.

THE SIMP FACTOR

When it comes to managing my finances—
the nuts and bolts of investments, budgets,
inflow and outgo—my psychological age
falls somewhere between Pampers and
Captain Kangaroo. I don't want to think
about money. It's boring, it's hard, it's scary
and *I won't do it.*

—Natalie Angier, author

Even though women have emerged from the Money Decade of the 1980s as the fastest growing part of the work force, even though many women manage their paychecks, what they know about finances is stuck back in the 1950s. "Women are still in a very transitional role in which a man makes the investment decisions," writes Marilyn Cohen, a principal of the firm Capital Insights. "I don't find the young urban professional woman who is married any more interested in money and investing than her mother who had a traditional housewife role. I find it very distressing."

I find it distressing as well. While women talk more easily about sex in marriage than they used to, I've found that many women, even the most successful managerial and professional women I've interviewed, are still hesitant to talk about money in marriage. They are more at ease discussing the intensity of their orgasms than the balance in their bank account.

These women appear to live double lives. On the job they are able to think analytically and clear-headedly, managing millions of their company's dollars without breaking a nail. But once women leave the office, they seem to take leave of their fiscal sanity and are somehow unable to face planning their own financial future. They're great at handling other people's money, but awful with their own. "Yes, yes, yes, we're terrific at our jobs and at handling other people's money," contends Connie S. P. Chen, of Chen Planning Consultants, Inc., a New York financial consulting firm. "But we don't always apply those terrific managerial skills to ourselves."

Although we are savvy at the office, when we get home we metamorphose into SIMP—the female equivalent of the male wimp. I'm referring to the "can't be bothered" attitude that many women have about finances. So many women told me sincerely that "money doesn't matter," that I stuck the tag SIMP on that myth in the hope that it will jar women into seeing how naive, how harmful, being a moneyphobic really is.

Beth, a woman I interviewed, is typical. Beth is a therapist in private practice, whose marriage is an equal partnership in all ways, with responsibilities shared and negotiable. She told me that she and her husband put "all our money in the same pot," and that they "discuss the budget together." But the picture changed when I asked her to rate herself in terms of how informed she was about where their money is invested and the details of her retirement plan. Beth suddenly looked self-conscious and admitted that she was "not very informed." I soon discovered that she isn't the only "not very informed" woman. Not at all.

"I suffer from a chronic case of financial phobia," says writer Natalie Angier. "All across America, thousands of women just like me—women who are proud of their independence and their success—turn into something the consistency of béarnaise sauce when faced with the prospect of choosing a corporate profit-sharing plan, examining a stock prospectus, closing a mortgage, or simply keeping track of the monthly bills."

By any measure of money smarts, Angier reports that "we women are nitwits compared to men." In a survey of 2,250 U.S. households conducted for *Money Magazine,* Lieberman Research of New York found that men are up to three times more likely to understand financial and business terms like "stock dividend," "prime rate," "hostile takeover," and "junk bond." The Lieberman survey also found that only about 20 percent of the women owned stocks and mutual funds (compared with more than 40 percent of the men), "preferring safer though less lucrative investments such as bank and money market accounts."

Women also seem to shy away from getting advice from financial professionals. "When I was working as an investment broker, very few younger women ever came to me," relates Anne Kohn Blau, coauthor of a recently published financial guide for women called *The Sex of the Dollar.* "A great many younger men came. They were anxious to learn about investments and how to put some money into the pot. I must admit I developed some very poor impressions of younger women's attitudes."

Before women can become more adept at dealing with their finances, we have to ask ourselves, "What is holding us back? Why, at the thought of planning for our financial future, do we come down with a money migraine, pull a Scarlett O'Hara, and tell ourselves, 'I'll think about it tomorrow?'"

Our queasiness about finances has little to do with hard cash. SIMP attitudes are not coincidental, they are the result of years of training. Look over your shoulder to our pink-painted nurseries, and it becomes clear why so many of us are not more comfortable about finances. Girls and boys are raised very differently when it comes to money. While boys learn about earnings and responsibility, girls are given lessons in looking good and getting along well with others. While young boys are told that someday they will grow up, get a good job, and support their families, young girls receive mixed messages about earning money. On one hand, we learn that money is good, and it's good to have money so that we can shop till we drop. At the same time we are taught that we need not clutter up our pretty little heads with money matters. Just marry well; select a man who is a good provider, and he will take care of your money worries. We have been led to believe that marriage, even if we work outside the home, is our real career. Even women who establish a career and haven't put their life on hold until they meet Mr. Right fall into the "he'll take care of me" mode when they do meet him.

Even if we yearned to build a megabuck conglomerate, where are the blueprints for women? In the media—the mirror in which we see ourselves—female financial wizards are mostly invisible or portrayed as Joan Crawford clones who count their millions by day and cry on their lonely pillows by night.

"We live with so many money myths," explains Olivia Mellan, a psychotherapist in Washington, D.C., who gives seminars on the psychology of money. "It equals love, happiness, self-worth, control. These equations are deep-rooted in our psyche, and it's very hard to undo them." We carry around such a crazy quilt of subconscious beliefs, emotions, fears, and superstitions about money that it's no wonder most women are spooked about finances.

Admittedly, women do have particular difficulty separating money from notions of love and femininity. Even the most independent of women may feel, deep down, the desire for a white knight or a Rhett Butler to rescue them from the hard realities of life. This could mean anything from straightening out the checkbook to managing the stock portfolio. And if and when this prince does arrive, the woman may find his comparatively greater knowledge of financial ins and outs so intimidating that she willingly gives up all control over her own income. "My husband is a stockbroker," relates my friend Alice. "He deals with investments every day. It's easier to let him deal with our money. Why should I do it when that's his business?"

Financial planners frequently encounter the same apathy among many of the working women in their clientele, most of whom are wealthy middle-aged executives. "Often," explains Michael Stein, "where you have two executives . . . the husband still tends to be the dominant one. A dominating woman is the exception more than the rule."

"I've seen very successful women who go home and turn their paychecks over to their husbands," writes Victoria Felton-Collins, a financial planner and psychologist, in her book *Couples and Money.* "They may manage millions of dollars for their companies, but when they get home it's a different story." In fact, for every couple making investment decisions jointly, there are many more who fail to plan jointly or even to discuss important financial matters.

There is nothing wrong with wanting to merge into an intimate relationship and pool money. The trouble arises when we link trust and love with money and neglect our finances in the name of love. All too often a woman has the fantasy that her husband is acting in her best interests. He may be, but that kind of unquestioning reliance on being taken care of can be disastrous. Not only does this notion conflict with the concept of equal partnership, it makes a woman vulnerable to serious financial problems if her marriage falls apart. The so-called equality of no-fault divorce laws and community property are blind to the economic inequality that still exists between men and women. This is the reality: Vast numbers of marriages end in divorce. A failed marriage is emotionally traumatic for any woman, but a woman with some financial acumen at least has an advantage when it comes to rebuilding her life.

"Often, it's not until death or divorce that women take a more active role in their financial futures," comments Jan Warners, a lawyer who runs a financial counseling service for women in Columbia, South Carolina. Warners estimates that three quarters of his female clients, most of whom are forty or older, come to him without the financial know-how needed to make it alone. "The average person who comes to us has been the victim of the demise of a fifteen- to twenty-year marriage with no business acumen because she has relied on someone else to do it. And we deal with some pretty good businesswomen."

Unfortunately, most women do not recognize this problem until they are drowning in it. Women are trained to think about others, not about "I," and certainly not about the fact that they need to have and understand money because it's what runs the country and their lives. When something goes wrong in their marriage, they may discover that whether they work or not, they are economically dependent on their husbands.

It is not only naive but self-defeating for women to cling to the romantic fantasy of being taken care of. A woman coming out of a marriage without the ability to adequately support herself, and without some form of back pay or compensation, is left with empty pockets. Even women who have worked for years can find themselves in financial trouble because their paycheck isn't really enough to live on, much less put something aside for cold winter nights.

Divorce is one of the prime culprits in the feminization of poverty. Widowhood is another factor. According to the American Association of Retired Persons (AARP), "almost three-fourths of elderly Americans living below the poverty level are women. And, half the widows who are poor now were not poor before their husbands died." These are cold, harsh statistics. Cold enough and harsh enough, I hope, to be a wake-up call for all of us who, for any reason, aren't paying attention to the fact that *money does matter.*

We may have less savvy because we lack power in our marriages to make financial decisions, or we may lack power because we lack knowledge about how to handle money. Whatever the cause/effect relationship may be, it is clear that we have to take control of our finances. A step in the right direction is to stop sashaying around trying to avoid financial responsibility. A good rule of thumb is to ask yourself what would happen if your relationship broke up—if you divorced, if he died, or if one or both of you were out of work or suffered a long, expensive health problem. If you don't know (and especially if your partner gives you a love pat and says, "Not to worry, I'm taking care of everything,") you need to worry and take charge of your life.

THE COLOR OF MONEY

There is nothing magic about number crunching, and nothing especially difficult about making our money work for us and getting a grip on our balance sheet. "You don't have to be versed in macroeconomics—the money supply, fiscal and monetary policies, interest-rate fluctuations, the Federal Reserve," advises financial planner Connie S. P. Chen. "What you really need to do is think microeconomically about your own financial needs."

And, lest we forget, we aren't really ignoramuses about money. We earn money. We work for a living. We do have the ability to manage money. We simply need to be as interested, as watchful, and as competent in managing our own money as we are budget-smart on the job.

The best way to overcome our traditional female phobia about personal finances is to do something concrete to get the most out of the money we earn. Don't expect an instant personality make-over from SIMP to fiscal sage. It took years for us to develop the attitudes we have about money, and it will take us a while to turn them around. Money managers advise us to take the following steps, one at a time.

Step One: Determine present and future needs and make out a budget you can live with. This means determining how much money you have, how much you must spend for essentials— mortgage, electricity, phone, food—and how much discretionary income remains. Be honest about what you earn and what you spend; covering up your spending habits is not only kidding yourself but actually cheating on yourself. Then, take another look at the budget to determine if there is any way to spend less on nonfixed items. If so, that's what you'll have to do. Forget about charging those red cowgirl boots you've been drooling over.

Step Two: Concentrate on one subject at a time when learning about personal finances. Figure out what small area of finance interests you, and learn as much as you can about that one subject. Then go on to something else. For instance, if you need car insurance, find out everything you can about what is offered and what's the best deal. You don't need to make up for all past fiscal failings at once. And you can't be an expert on everything. Think of how you can dazzle someone at the next office get-together by dropping a few references to the status of the bond market.

Step Three: Become actively involved in the management of your money—both your own and the pooled resources of your marriage. Find a financial adviser you can trust, and get some guidance on plotting the big picture. (Ask people who seem to be smart about money whom they use, and then check up on that person's track record.)

The good news is that there's a lot of help out there. Browse through the personal finance section of your favorite bookstore. Check out the classes at your local college. Attend seminars given by investment firms. Go to the library and read about getting money-smarter through magazines and books. In the Financial Management Resources section at the back of this book I've listed some sources that I have found to be especially helpful, as well as some that financial advisers recommend.

On an encouraging note, money managers say that younger women are becoming better informed about some aspects of finances, especially workplace retirement plans. In fact, I see the glass of women's money situation as half full, not half empty. As women continue to move up in the work force and gain confidence about earning and managing money, we'll bring home more than our paychecks—we'll bring home much greater power and independence.

But the best news that the financial analysts, psychologists, and former financial phobics bring to the table is this: no matter how tight your budget is and how little you know about managing money, there is hope for you. I know, because I was a SIMP once myself. Now, I even enter all of my ATM cash withdrawals in my checkbook and balance it on the spot. I've learned that when you take control of your money, you feel like a grown-up, one who is a full equal partner in love *and* money. Your bonus? Go buy those red cowgirl boots—for cash.

6

WHEN SHE EARNS
MORE THAN HE

He is wearing an expensive three-piece suit; she is wearing an expensive two-piece suit and carrying a briefcase. She surprises him with the gift of a diamond ring! "Why not?" the ad asks. "Give him a diamond. The gift of love from a woman to the man in her life."

Two great-looking, slenderer-than-slender women are putting on makeup and chatting. One confides that not only does her man think it's just great that she earns more money than he, but he also drinks *her* brand of scotch.

If commercials like these were an accurate reflection of life in the 1990s, it would be safe to assume that men are not threatened—that men, in fact, revel in knowing their spouses or lovers earn more money than they.

Don't bet on it. The only thing it is safe to assume is that money does matter, and it matters a lot. "Being equally successful seems to lead to the greatest life and relationship satisfaction for both women and men," reports a *Working Woman* magazine survey about success. However, the article goes on to say, "In the absence of equal success, the old standard prevails. For men, being the less successful one is a problem; for women, being the more successful one is a problem."

Logically, the fact that she is earning more money should be a bonus; the more money, the merrier. But the "problem" of her being the more successful one has little to do with logic. Money is the battlefield upon which many a power struggle between a man and a woman is waged. Money is a metaphor for power—who is in charge, who decides—and when a woman earns more money than her partner it adds new land mines to an already hazardous marital landscape.

The rough terrain a relationship faces when a woman has the fatter paycheck can be traced directly back to deeply rooted sex-role prescriptions—our sexual wiring. Men and women alike grow up learning that masculine men are *supposed* to earn more money and feminine women are *supposed* to be taken care of. The scenario may vary slightly, but the end result is the same.

The reversal of the good provider role has a profound effect on men who earn less than their wives. Traditional roles and attitudes die hard. Even the most contemporary of males is reluctant to yield the power and control that tradition has accorded the breadwinning man of the family, regardless of whether or not he earns most of the family income. Women, too, experience conflicting feelings; while they feel entitled to more power and control at home, they often resent not being taken care of. This much is certain: the powerful expectations about manhood and womanhood create obstacles for us as we try to work out the financial details and distribution of power involved in being equal partners.

Let's consider for a moment whether you need to concern yourself with this issue of women earning more than their partners. Statistically speaking, is it likely that you are in this situation now, or ever will be? Yes and no. Women who out-earn the men in their lives are not rare, but they aren't your average garden variety either.

According to the U.S. Bureau of the Census, the wife earns more than the husband in only one of every five dual-income marriages. And, of that group, only seven percent earn significantly more. (Unfortunately, the Bureau's criterion for *significantly* isn't clear.) Even if you aren't one of those women who earns more than her man, you may be on a career track that will take you in that direction. Give yourself time.

Being on a high-profile career track is not the only reason why a woman may be the couple's higher wage earner. Her partner could be ill, in school, or in a training program. For other women, their breadwinning status is linked to our downsizing economy. As more and more men are laid off or forced to retire early, more and more women are becoming the family's primary or sole means of support. This situation could confront any of us, given America's uncertain economic future. It is possible that you may become the one who brings home most, or all, of the bacon whether you want to or not.

Meanwhile, the more you know about how higher-earning women deal with their intimate relationships, the more insight you will have about your own situation, should you ever need it. The best approach is to face the issues squarely; to look at why the reversal of breadwinning roles threatens both men and women and how the resulting competition for power can cripple the relationship.

Clearly, being on a faster track than your lover can test the dynamics of a relationship. But as you will see, men and women can and do alter the basic fabric of a partnership to fit their own unique situation. And a good first step in that direction is to remember that you don't have to leave your effectiveness in dealing with our changing gender roles and responsibilities at the office; you can carry this skill with you when you enter the front door of your home.

I spoke with a number of high-profile women who have adapted their on-the-job management skills to improve their intimate partnership. Although these women can't offer guaranteed solutions to the problems you may encounter, it is helpful to know that there are positive ways to navigate those less-traveled roads to equality in an intimate relationship.

THE DYNAMICS OF THE GOOD PROVIDER ROLE

I think men are caught in between two powerful and conflicting ideas. On the one hand, intellectually we buy into the idea that it is terrific having a successful wife. On the other, we were raised to believe that being the family breadwinner is what makes a man a man.

—Dennis, pharmacist

It's difficult for women to understand why men relate so strongly to the traditional idea that they must be a good provider. Women characteristically assert that "Work is what I do, not what I am," while men typically offer their occupation first when asked about themselves.

A man's work and his ability to provide for his family have long been his identification with maleness. He is what he does. Men are judged as men by the living they provide, not just for themselves but for their families. According to sociologist Sheldon Demos, over the past decades "to be a man one had to be not only a provider but a *good* provider. Success in the good-provider role came in time to define masculinity itself. The good provider had to achieve, to win, to succeed, to dominate. He was the BreadWINNER. He had to show strength, cunning, inventiveness, endurance—a whole range of traits henceforth defined as exclusively 'masculine.'" Men were judged by a standard "that endows a money-making man with sexiness and virility, and is based on men's dominance, strength, and ability to care for 'his' woman." The central core of a man's life, the very touchstone of his manhood, was his role as the family provider. Researcher Roger Gould reminds us that not so long ago, when a wife earned a good salary she was thought to be not just taking over the man's role but "co-opting the man's passport to masculinity and he was effectively castrated." That is one powerful image!

It's no wonder then, as Francis Roe explains, "The effort involved in getting men to give up their belief that they must be the head of the household can be compared to that involved in deprogramming a cult member."

Despite those powerful cultural forces at play, a subtle revolution has been taking place as vast numbers of women enter the labor force and move up the wage-earning scale: the good-provider role with its prerogatives and privileges is becoming diluted. The death knell was rung on men's breadwinner role in 1980 when the U.S. Census no longer automatically assumed that the male member of the household was its head. These changes in family structure affect women very differently than they do men because men and women have such different vantage points with regard to marriage and family. The alterations for women have been clear-cut—getting jobs, having more legal options both inside and outside of the family, experiencing less overt discrimination, watching educational gates open. By and large, these changes have an upbeat, take-hold-of-your-life quality about them. For men, however, the transformations typically consist of diffused feedback effects of what is happening to women. And let's be honest: the changes usually involve men in some sort of decline in terms of the traditional concepts of male power and status.

Still, the idea of man-as-provider has hardly gone by the wayside. Living by a new pattern of roles can be fraught with tension, even for those couples who are committed to the demise of the male breadwinner role, as Leonard and Katharine discovered. Katharine recently was promoted to publisher for a major newspaper chain, putting her in a new income bracket. Leonard, a management professor, explains, "Katharine and I have always considered our dual careers as a partnership, and we always do what is best for the partnership." But he admits it can be tough for a man when a woman takes such a prominent position in the community. There was some questioning from his male friends, "Gee, Len . . . How do you feel about your wife making so much more money than you?" Leonard concedes that it feels "odd," and that it takes a major adjustment within and outside of their partnership. "We are still working on it," he resignedly concludes.

Dan is a Presbyterian minister who left New York and came to Los Angeles to accompany his wife Victoria when she became head minister of a large congregation. Dan was dismayed by the reactions that arose from his relocation. He experienced "strange feelings" he recalls, when he found himself "known at social gatherings as the husband of Victoria." He also was the target of jibes in the locker room at the gym: "Who's following whose career?"

"First, I kind of joked back," Dan says. "Then I didn't joke back. My response was usually, 'Well, it puts bread on the table.'" But he adds, "These reactions can catch you off guard because it can destroy your self-esteem. You start to look at your job and wonder, 'Do *I* have a career?'"

A brave new world, indeed. Men relocating for their spouse's careers? Our old guidelines for a successful relationship simply don't apply. Yet when we observe the everyday events around us, it looks more like the old than the new. It's maddening, but we are foolish if we brush aside the power of traditional, good-provider sex-role training too quickly. In trying to define and fulfill new roles when the woman is a primary breadwinner, men and women find themselves competing for power rather than providing each other with the support and love that one expects and needs from a partnership.

COMPETITION: WHO IS KEEPING SCORE?

Of all the dynamics involved in adjusting to the realities of two-career marriages, the one that is most destructive to the soul of the relationship is men's uneasiness about "who's on top." This bent for competition can pit mates against each other in terms of who works harder, who gets more attention or more publicity in the media, who has higher status within his or her occupation, who has the greater authority. Lisa Silberstein, a psychologist at Yale University, discovered when she was researching her doctoral dissertation on dual-career couples that competition "was just too hot a topic for couples to discuss frankly. It caused the most squirming among the twenty couples I interviewed. It's a taboo subject because women can't experience it without conflict and men don't want to compete with women, especially with their spouses." Maybe men don't want to compete with their spouses on a conscious level, but they tend to view their wife's success as something that takes away from their own. Men don't always recognize how much of their personality and self-esteem are wrapped up in being not just successful, but more successful than the woman they love. They rarely acknowledge how much more likely they are than their wives to feel competitive within the marriage.

Women simply don't understand men's overriding competitive urge to surpass their mate; we were not raised to believe that our womanhood depended upon the size of our paycheck. But men are trained to be competitive. Journalist Pete Hamill elaborates, "From childhood, they are told they can be anything in this country: center fielder for the Yankees, head of the Chrysler Corporation, President of the United States. They are trained to compete. On the playing field. In class. At their first jobs." One of the most visible marks of success is how much money the man has won by triumphing over other men. It's the law of the economic jungle. The images of male success do not portray men washing dishes, changing diapers, or clipping coupons. It's the toys, the cars, and the bank accounts that matter.

So doesn't it make sense that a man would be happiest with a very successful wife—a woman who makes a lot of money and provokes envy among his peers? On the surface, this seems to be the case. Philip Blumstein and Pepper Schwartz, authors of *American Couples,* report that most of the husbands they studied were happier married to successful, working wives. These men said they were happy because their wives' ambitions fired their own. But read the fine print. A great number of husbands reported being unhappy if their wives were more ambitious or successful than they. They feared their wives' careers could eventually come before their own—one thing they didn't want to happen.

For many men the rewards of having a wage-earning partner are mitigated by viewing her as a competitor for status, money, and power. Blumstein and Schwartz add that a wife's success "pleases her husband only if he is doing well himself. When his wife's success surpasses his, his home is no longer his castle—a safe haven from competition—but just another reminder of what he perceives to be his inadequacies in the marketplace." No matter how well a man is doing in his career, he worries that his partner may be doing better. A promotion, a raise, or a special compliment from a supervisor are the clear and standard signs of accomplishment. But these pleasures may be short-lived if he discovers that his achievement pales in comparison with someone else's. In a two-paycheck household, the person he compares himself with may be his partner. Josh, a marketing director, describes this tendency. "I like the fact that my wife is an engineer," he says, "but I have real trouble with her earning a little more money than I do because she gets annual bonuses. I don't consider her income as breadwinning. I consider my career to be the most important and myself to be the real provider. It's not rational, but there it is." Josh's feelings, like those of many other men, tend to be governed by a notion deeply entrenched in our society—that the man in a marriage is the primary financial provider and thus the primary power broker. When that's not the case, many men feel threatened.

Even when a man is philosophically committed to egalitarianism in marriage, living by a new pattern of breadwinning can strain a relationship to its limits. Adjusting to new roles and competing for old ones can threaten even the strongest partnership when there are no guidelines to follow. As men step down from or share their coveted positions in the household, and women face uncomfortable new responsibilities and privileges, there are bound to be pressures. These pressures can lead to the loss of some very valuable perks of a marriage—emotional support, cooperation, and mutual respect. These may be replaced by resentment, hostility, and competitiveness.

June, an investment banker, recalls how her success was on a collision course with her husband's competitiveness until she took action to avoid a crash. In her words, "On one level Marc understood that my career is important and that it took a lot of effort and concentration. But on the other hand, he got his nose out of joint because I got so much recognition. I know that his feelings of envy were difficult for him (and may still be). But I know he only wants the best for me and he wouldn't wish me any kind of failure or setback. He desires more for himself, not less for me.

"He didn't put hurdles in my path but he didn't offer much moral support, or much of anything else, either. He never picked me up from the airport, or planned anything special for me when I had been out of town. The night I knew things had to change was the night I got home from a trip with a bad case of the flu. I could barely walk (I slumped) through the front door, and all he did was grunt in my general direction. He was watching TV and didn't even get up. I asked him to please get my suitcase out of my car and carry it upstairs for me. He could hardly tear himself away from the TV but he finally did it, although he acted as if it were a great imposition. I was so angry that I knew we had to resolve the problem or get a divorce. I didn't want a divorce. But it took me several days while I recouped from the flu to think over my situation.

"For one thing, I knew I wouldn't put up with someone at my office harboring resentment toward me over my achievements. I simply won't allow a passive-aggressive relationship at the office to fester. If one of my peers or employees has a complaint or a problem with me I expect them to place it on the table so we can discuss it. I've learned from different office situations that you have to confront people who carry a grudge or who have something on their minds they are angry with you about, but who don't speak up. I've also learned that the complaint isn't always objective, but sometimes subjective. Whether their gripe with you is logical or not, though, it is still 'real.'

"When I landed my biggest account, my coworker Doris began to drop sarcastic remarks around the office about my 'luck.' I knew I had to call for a real heart-to-heart to clear the air if we were to continue to work together. In the same light, I had to face up to the realization that Marc's bottled-up competitive feelings were eroding our marriage. To put it bluntly, I was getting progressively fed up with his behavior.

"Just as I did with Doris, I set up a time to talk to Marc. I told him, in advance, that the topic would be our drifting apart since my promotion. Past experience has taught me to be straightforward and give the other person an idea of what it is you want to discuss in advance. When the issue on the table is a delicate one, or a controversial one, it's better not to 'spring' the topic on the person; it's better to give them some time to think things over.

"When we met, instead of identifying the 'issue' as that I earn more money, I focused the discussion on how he felt about our situation and why he felt that way. Then I told him how his actions made me feel. I adhered to the basics of good communication: I didn't blame; I didn't go into a tirade about his lousy attitude. We kept focused on 'how can we deal with this competitive thing.' The truth is that it is very likely that I will continue to out-earn him, so we have to learn to deal with that reality.

"We decided that we both have to make adjustments. I agreed to stop expecting him to welcome me home like my mom would. He agreed to revise his notion that being kind and considerate makes him look like a wimp: 'I'm her loyal servant because she earns more money.' (I had no idea that he felt he was treated like an underling when I expected some special TLC.) It's not as easy as I'm making it sound. He will never enjoy being the lesser-wage earner.

"At work you have to accept that there will always be employees who feel competitive and resentful about another person's promotion. If that competitive feeling is directed at you, the best thing to do is confront the issue head on. Do lunch; have a meeting; do whatever it takes. Just find a quiet time and place and then insist on dealing with the problem. Ask the other person to put their cards out on the table, and you do the same. You can't deal with a negative situation unless it is out in the open."

June's strategy for dealing with another person's competitive passive-aggressive behavior is helpful—both at the office and at home. Experts in settling disputes agree that the only way to resolve a simmering issue is to bring it up to the surface for examination. Antagonistic emotions that are deeply felt but mostly camouflaged can cause as much disharmony as verbal expressions of anger or frustration. Acknowledging that something is amiss is a major step forward.

If a coworker or employee who has been contentious with you bristled when you suggested a meeting to clear the air, you wouldn't back off, would you? So don't be intimidated if your partner acts prickly. Be persistent. You might say, "I value our relationship and we can't afford not to talk about this issue."

Let your partner know how you perceive the situation, and be supportive of his feelings without coddling him. Psychotherapist

Sonya Rhodes notes that "the trick is to focus on your own feelings, starting off with 'I feel' rather than 'you always.' Using this approach, you can criticize in the right spirit and touch on a mate's hot spots— super-sensitive psychic areas—without burning him or yourself."

Stick to the task at hand. Establish a dialogue by calmly stating your feelings and asking questions. Identify the problem from both of your perspectives and then work out an approach you both agree on to resolve the problem.

If this doesn't work, Rhodes suggests, "let it go for now and see whether he initiates a discussion later. Sometimes a spouse who first resists an open give-and-take conversation will mull the issue over and raise it himself when ready. If he doesn't bring the issue up again, you can, at a time when you're both feeling relaxed and communicative."

THE FRAGILE MALE EGO

On the flip side of the male competitive assertive edge is the fragile male ego. If a man grew up in a family with a stalwart, bread-winning father and a mother who admired his father as the good provider, his partner's higher-earning profile can make him feel insecure, anxious, and depressed. In a word, inadequate.

Men have been judged by the size of their wallets for so long that they fear they won't be loved if theirs is slimmer than their mate's. Men usually don't expose this tender soft spot on their egos to their partner, so we often miss or misunderstand what they are feeling. And these miscues are serious barriers to having the kind of partnership we want. A man's depression over feeling inadequate can erode the good feelings between partners just as lethally as competitive passive-aggressive power plays.

Take the case of Margie and her spouse, James. Margie, a medical malpractice lawyer, went from a small practice to a thriving law firm in a very short time. James is a free-lance writer and part-time instructor at a college. Although he has done well it is still, as he puts it, "slim pickings." Reflecting further, he continues, "Sometimes I feel like a house husband. I feel as though I am a deadbeat because I'm not a partner in the financial sense. I found it difficult because for years we earned pretty much the same; now there is a big difference. I'm doing better but still not in Margie's league."

James's feelings about the disparity in their incomes were taking their toll on the good relationship they always had. Margie observes, "We've been married for eight years and for the last two, because of settling some big cases, my earnings have jumped off the charts. Unless something major happens I'm going to be doing even better over the next ten years. He tries not to show it, but I know it bothers him. I don't expect him to earn a lot of money. He might strike it big someday but if not, it doesn't matter to me. I enjoy his writing and take pride in seeing his work. But things between us were on shaky ground. I couldn't enjoy my own success because I felt I had to downplay everything I was doing at work."

Margie realized that she had to do something to change the atmosphere at home. She found it "depressing" and "demeaning" to pretend that all was well "by tiptoeing around his ego." She recognized that quitting her job or putting it on the back burner was *not* for her. The approach she took was one of directly confronting the issue.

"Last year I had to deal with my secretary, who was very unhappy and distraught over troubles in her marriage. The office was slowly falling apart because she was so distracted. But when I would try to bring the topic of her being distracted up for discussion she would deny having any problems at all. Finally I had to take action and get her to stop denying that she was deeply troubled and needed help. I set up a meeting and was very direct about how her problems in her personal life were affecting the office. I'm not a therapist and I don't think a supervisor should give personal advice or get too involved in an employee's personal life. My role was to acknowledge that I perceived a problem existed and let her know I valued her good mental health. I recommended different avenues of help and she was receptive. After a while she bounced back, and was as efficient as she had always been. It's not so easy to bring up a delicate issue when the other person would rather not discuss it. But it's been my experience that these situations rarely improve on their own.

"I used the same straightforward approach with James that I use at my office to help someone come to terms with having a problem that is interfering with their job. In this case, it was our marriage. We went out to dinner and I asked him point-blank to discuss his feelings about my income being greater than his. He said it was no problem. But I wouldn't settle for that. I told him it seemed to me that something was troubling him, and I felt it was the difference in our earnings. He finally admitted that it was a difficult issue for him. We talked about the positive and negative side to my being the main breadwinner. I had to admit that it would be nice if he did earn more money. But he doesn't, and I enjoy being ambitious and bringing in a fat paycheck. He admitted that he did feel inadequate at times and wished he were a greater financial success. That discussion opened the door for us. James still has to work out his inner conflicts over not being the great provider, but things have improved. I feel as if we've forded a dangerous creek together. We made it over a major hurdle, and we are still together."

It's a cliché, but it's true: you can't solve anyone's problems but your own. You can't kiss away a boo-boo and, voilà, the other person's inner conflicts or despair evaporate. Even if you are very skilled at interpersonal communication, there is a limit to how much you can do to help your partner come to terms with something that is gnawing away at him. One way to deal with the issue, recommends New York therapist Nancy Arann, is to "respect boundaries"—his and yours. Arann explains, "You can offer emotional support, but only he can do something about it. You have to give yourself permission to enjoy your career without feeling guilty, without feeling responsible for him—or being flooded by his crisis."

Margie agrees. "I had to face up to the fact that I could be loving and understanding, but in the end he had to deal with his feelings on his own terms in his own way. You can be supportive, but in the end you can't pump up someone else." However, you can take an assertive approach, as Margie did, and discuss how your partner's feelings of being compromised or inadequate are taking away from the joy of being together. By confronting the fragile-ego issue with James, she enabled them to honestly work out a way to live with their lopsided earnings. If nothing else, direct communication brings you one step closer to dealing with your partnership as it really is, not as it used to be.

In spite of all I've said above, I don't want to leave you with the impression that overcoming the obstacles to equal partnership when the woman is earning more money than her partner is a simple matter of men taming their competitive, good-provider urges or confronting the fragile nature of the male ego. Women have their own egos and demons to deal with.

STARING DOWN THE "BITCH-GODDESS" OF SUCCESS

Because it goes against the grain of the breadwinner/good wife dynamic, when a woman earns a higher income than her partner she often finds herself downplaying her salary. Anne Fisher, writing about the top money-making women in America, reports that the stereotype lingers that real women aren't concerned about making money. "I would have thought that we'd come far enough by now to make a lot of money and be comfortable about it . . . but there still is a real social stigma attached to women making a lot of money." And that stigma isn't just something that men attach to women earning money. Women do it, too.

Lurking deep within our feminine being, we harbor the same belief about men that we did years ago when we twirled in front of the mirror in a pastel party dress dreaming of the day we would meet Mr. Perfect. He would, *should,* be taller, make a lot of money, and have loads of savvy and charm. It's all we have ever been taught to look for in a man. We read about it in romance novels, see it at the movies and on television. It's the stuff fairy tales and soap operas are made of.

It's never easy to break with tradition, but it's a lot harder when you're ambivalent about wanting to make that break. We wear the mantle of success—what William James so creatively described as the "bitch-goddess"—very uneasily. The crux of the issue is this: *we really don't think a woman ought to earn more money than her mate.* In our hearts, we believe a real man takes care of his woman. So when we earn more than he, we are likely to feel unfeminine, guilty, or unloved.

We cover up our real feelings by denying them. It's personally painful. It's politically incorrect. How does a competent woman with a responsible fast-track career admit, even to herself, that she doesn't believe she ought to be higher on the totem pole than her mate? "It's embarrassing to admit you have this sneaky little feeling you shouldn't be earning more than your husband, that there's something wrong with it," explains Baila Zeitz, a psychologist who has done extensive research on two-career couples.

Embarrassing or not, those old teachings stubbornly cling to our psyche despite the changes in our external world. How could it possibly be otherwise? The stereotype of the male as the princely breadwinner and captain of our ship is not just drummed into the male, it is what we ourselves learned at our mother's and father's knees. Although practically every woman knows differently in her head, many still find themselves buying into it.

While we are loath to admit it, it is very difficult for some women to fully respect a man as her equal partner if he doesn't live up to, at least to a sizable degree, the cultural macho image of protector and provider. A man who loves us takes care of us. Right?

MORE THAN WE BARGAINED FOR

I thought as I got stronger, he would get stronger. I didn't think he would get weaker! He has become passive and doesn't mind at all that I'm the only one going out to swim with the sharks.

—Shelly, executive director
of a health agency

A good measure of our own attitude about the male being the primary breadwinner is how we view the possibility of our spouse quitting work or getting a lesser-paying job than ours. In most married couples, if the woman wanted to quit working and it was financially feasible, her husband would probably acquiesce. Conversely, if the man wants to quit working or doesn't shoulder the main financial burden for the family, he may lose some respect in the eyes of his wife. We might not say it, but we would surely think that in a cavalier or Peter Pan fashion he was abandoning his responsibilities.

While women increasingly view employment as vital to their well-being and self-esteem, they still want to preserve men's traditional commitment to the world of work. As Blumfield and Schwartz found, "When women succeed in the world of work, they do not want him to leave or slow down. Women want to look up to, or at least directly across at, their partner to respect him." In short, a man who would want to quit working, or even be content to come in second in the earning competition with his partner, is a man we judge to be flawed. Women tell me they don't like themselves for feeling this way, but there it is.

The notion that a man must be the breadwinner has a long reach. It can even influence a woman's satisfaction with her job. For instance, some working wives, while enjoying their status and the money they earn, feel cheated at the marriage game. Because their income is needed, they are denied options that women without breadwinning responsibilities enjoy, such as taking time out from a career to care for children or pursue other interests.

Witness Dina, a video store manager. "When I married Steve he had a great job in an insurance firm. But one day out of the blue Steve tells me he wants to quit his job because he hates it. He always wanted to go into public radio as a producer. Well, he had to go back to school for two years and then had to intern at a station. (Interns don't get paid.) I have had to deal with a lot of anger about my situation. On one hand, I am happy that Steve is doing what he wants to do. On the other, I feel tricked in a way. I don't know if I would have married him if I had known he would be content to earn so little money. It sounds awful, but I was a lot happier knowing I wasn't responsible for being the one to succeed and make us comfortable in our old age."

As Dina's experience illustrates, when a man jumps off the fast track it can be a struggle for us to reconcile our hopes, ambitions, and desires with those of our mates. But that kind of struggle pales next to the crisis of a partner's unemployment. As numbers of men are being laid off or forced to retire early, more wage-earning wives are becoming the family's primary—or sole—means of support. We signed on for cobreadwinner, but if we end up taking on the entire financial and psychological role ourselves, it's a whole different ball game. "Many working women are surprised by their own reaction when their husband loses his job," advises Ruth Rosenbaum, a therapist in private practice. "They believed that they really didn't care about the man supporting them or being a provider. But when he is out of work, hidden issues come to the surface. Sometimes, if a woman hasn't thought through what she expects and wants of her husband, the rules can suddenly change midstream without his even knowing it, or her admitting it. He thought he married a liberated woman, but suddenly he finds that security is her top priority." If the two were never on equal footing as breadwinners—say, if he earned twice as much as she and the agreement from the beginning was that his career was more important—it's even more problematic.

Dr. Judith Sills suggests that even the most self-sufficient and successful working woman can feel trapped in the breadwinner role. "You know you are supposed to be supportive, positive, and optimistic, but you often feel resentful and envious," Sills informs us. "Many women still maintain the fantasy that they wouldn't have to work—that their husbands could take care of them: 'I'm married, so I could quit my job anytime. Of course, I wouldn't, but . . .' When he loses his job, that fantasy of freedom is broken."

Warren Farrell, author of *Why Men Are the Way They Are*, asserts that we have transferred the old fantasy of being saved by a man from having to work, to the fantasy of having the option of working or not working. Farrell explains, "When we picture a working woman, we picture a woman who has outgrown the primary fantasy that a man will support her. In fact . . . the married woman who works because her husband earns too little only strengthens the fantasy of a husband who earns more. . . . Many more women are working and providing for themselves, but very few women have changed their expectations of men, and very few women expect themselves to support men for even a part of their lives, except to go to graduate school to make them better breadwinners."

Clearly the attitudes of women, as well as the attitudes of men, contribute to the tension in relationships of breadwinning or higher-earning women. "Sometimes women trap themselves in the old macho pattern even more than men do," explains therapist Rosenbaum. "Because of the way we were all raised, it's very easy, even for an independent, financially self-sufficient woman, to feel a loss of security and a loss of love when he isn't the breadwinner."

It's not easy for a woman to give up the fantasy of being taken care of, and it's not easy for men to give up the perks of being the primary breadwinner. No matter how many psychological pretzel-bends we do, liberating ourselves from our girlish training takes time, and it takes practice.

It helps to remember that your goal is to be a treasured equal partner with the man you love. Too often the sense of shared values and the agreement to be equal partners gets lost in the upheaval of the loss of a job. Most couples need to reaffirm the original contract they had when they became partners. In most cases this means recognizing that the woman has always planned on working, rather than being economically dependent on her spouse. And it helps to stay aware of the checks and balances of an equal partnership. Her present status as a sole wage-earner rather than a co-wage-earner is (one hopes) not a permanent situation.

The case of Joe, a former TV anchorman, illustrates this situation. Joe relocated from Florida to North Carolina with his wife Bethany when she took a job directing an uptown redevelopment project there. "It's tough," laments Joe. "Sometimes I see my wife go off to work. I get panicky. I think, 'My God, what have I done?'"

Currently Joe is a house husband, spending his days making beds, doing laundry, making plans for a move into a new home, and thinking about his future. "We had an understanding when we married two years ago that we would support each others' career moves," he explains. Bethany had followed him to Florida, and now he feels it is his turn to be the follower.

It's the first time Joe can remember not having a job; maybe that's the reason he cannot quite relax. He admits it bothers him if people react strangely when he tells them he is a house husband. "They usually say, 'Come on, what do you do?'"

But Joe has Bethany's support—psychological as well as financial. She says she wants Joe to take his time deciding what he wants to do next. "This is the perfect opportunity for him to explore his options. I want him to be absolutely certain he does what he wants, whether it's going back into television or going back to school. We knew when we got married this would be a give-and-take marriage."

THE PRIMA DONNA REFLEX

There is another twist to how a woman's greater success affects her intimate partnership. Strangely enough, in most cases even when a woman earns a great deal more money than her mate, she doesn't necessarily acquire a proportionate amount of decision-making power in the partnership. This frustration over not getting a fair deal sets up the dynamics I tag a "prima donna reflex," an emotional backlash in response to the fact that no matter what she earns, she doesn't have equality.

Julie heads a prestigious medical library and earns substantially more than her husband Kevin, a graduate student and part-time manager of a popular restaurant chain. Julie is unhappy with this situation, not because of their unequal paychecks, but because of the unequal responsibility at home. She confesses, "There are times when I come home from work expecting the kind of dinner and clean house the traditional breadwinner always had. It peeves me that he doesn't take on more responsibilities for the daily maintenance because he doesn't have the major responsibility for providing for us. Now that I earn more money I'm not proud to say that I sometimes think I should have the bigger say about what goes on. I find myself thinking like a 'husband.'"

Other women who are primary breadwinners admit to sharing the same dilemma. Sandra is a case in point. A computer programmer, Sandra lives with Matthew, a real estate broker. Since the real estate market has been flat where they live in Arizona, Matthew has been home a lot and working what amounts to less than part-time. "There are times I get very angry over housework," Sandra complains. "I think, why aren't the kitchen and the bedroom cleaned? He's here all day. If I had some extra time home from work, I'd have cleaned out the closets and lined all of the kitchen shelves!"

Based on their status as primary breadwinners, women like Julie and Sandra would like to receive some of the same privileges of rank that men have always had as the family provider—to be catered to, given the best chair, awarded the plumpest piece of chicken. "To be," as Julie describes, "pampered the way my dad got taken care of by my mom!"

It's not so much that women expect to be treated as royalty because they earn good money. In fact, while women may think about demanding the privileges of rank, they rarely express those thoughts because it's more a fantasy than a need. They don't really want, or expect, their spouse to snap to attention and fetch their slippers. In actuality, women don't want to dominate their men any more than men want to be dominated.

What makes a woman have power-hungry urges is the realization that although she is earning the biggest portion of wages, she still is basically thrown into the role of the homemaker. The issue for many higher-salaried women is that men, even when they earn less, often act as if they are still the proverbial head of the household and expect to be waited on and taken care of as their dads were.

Women haven't been able to turn men's thinking around on the issue of shared power. Men have a long tradition of feeling they have the right to exercise control if they have proven their worth by being financially successful. It's not mere coincidence that husbands who have superior incomes and financial resources have held court at home. But because women have a short history of earning good money, they haven't acquired the knack of using their financial power to get their fair share of power in their intimate relationship. The evidence? Many higher-earning women cater to their partners' whims and do most of the housework, just as lesser-earning women do.

The balance of power will change when women recognize the potential and actual power of their economic clout. Anthony Astrachan, in his book *How Men Feel,* distills the situation for us. "Women traditionally see money as a matter of security; today they also associate it with autonomy, which is only a short step from power. As women become more familiar with the world of work for pay, they become more and more willing to make money the measure of power and to do the measuring themselves. That produces new anxieties in many men. Women's readiness to use money as a yardstick increases as their earnings rise, and men increasingly combine anxiety with anger and fear. The male emotions proliferate and intensify further when a woman consistently earns more money than her man, making him feel he has lost the male edge."

Rather than pretend that nothing much will change when women achieve financial parity with men, we are better off telling it like it is. As women do earn more money, men will indeed lose their male edge—the traditional perks of power based on the good-provider role. Women certainly will expect to have more decision-making power in their relationships than they've had traditionally.

Witness Monica, a CPA. "Money [who earns more] isn't so much the issue in my marriage," she declares. "Spending it—that was our problem. Although we commingle our money, I earn slightly more than he does. He is a typical depression kid (raised during the 1930s) and hates to spend money or see it spent. It was very annoying, and it's a source of tension that he has to comment on everything I buy. The house could be falling down around him but he ignores it. Upkeep is not in his vocabulary. After living with drapes that fell apart at the dry cleaners, I decided I had enough of trying to placate him. It took me too long to arrive at this point, but

I now act on my right to enjoy the fruits of *my* labor. I don't throw it in his face that it is 'my money' to spend as I see fit, tempting though it is.

"After the drape debacle, I knew I had to assert myself. I am, after all, a mature person trained to manage money. Once I accepted the fact that he and I would never agree about the need to buy anything, I felt a wave of calmness about the situation. I gave up trying to justify my actions and don't ask his permission to buy something I think is necessary. When he questions me about a purchase, I count to ten and calmly tell him I made the decision to buy it and feel it was the right decision. I don't justify what I buy anymore. What's he going to do? Take it back?

"The more self-assured I became, the less he questioned me. It's the same dynamics in my profession. You have to exude self-confidence in order for your clients to trust you. I had to assure Justin that I did use judgment about money and that I shared his same concern about being broke.

"If I acted apologetic and unsure of my financial decisions at the office I wouldn't last a day. When you handle people's money they expect you to be knowledgeable and confident about the decisions you make. Our relationship improved immensely after I stopped whining about not being able to spend my own money. Now I act on my belief that I deserve to have nice things and live in a comfortable home. As Cybill Shepherd says in the L'Oreal ads, 'I'm worth it.'"

What spurred Monica on to take an assertive stance was her confidence that she deserved the right to equal decision-making power in her relationship. Like Brenda, we have to respect and value what we know and who we are. As one woman expressed it with the kind of humor and self-confidence we all could use more of, "I make decisions at the office from nine to five and I think it would be a little strange if I came home and acted like a pussycat."

ACCEPTING SUCCESS

A lesson I've learned from talking to couples is that we can't assume that all men are programmed to find high-achieving women threatening; many men do overcome traditional prejudices and recognize the desirability (and the added economic safety net) of a woman who is truly an equal partner in all respects. There are men who can and do take pride in knowing that their wife has talents and wisdom that are greatly appreciated by many other people. Julie Connelly, writing for *Fortune* magazine, interviewed seventy managerial men with executive wives to see how their marriages fared. She found a mixture of confusion and cooperation in men adjusting to a nontraditional partnership, and she also found men who were supportive and admiring of their wives. The survivors of these executive marriages all agree on one point: "They work best when no one keeps score." Rod Hills, who is married to Carla Hills, the U.S. Trade Representative, remarked, "You invest where you can get the best return. For a long time I was the better investment than Carla was. If you look at our lives, the only thing that kept the marriage together was that we each did our share."

Connelly discovered that, as in other aspects of our changing profile of marriage, humor helps. Richard Blum, who is married to Diane Feinstein, the U.S. Senator from California, explained how he handles it when people call him Mr. Feinstein. "I tell them I prefer to go by my maiden name," he remarked.

It's not only the men who need to rethink their roles. It behooves us to examine our own attitudes as well. Someday our prince may come (or maybe he has already arrived), and we'll discover that he isn't likely to be as materially successful as we are. Accepting this change in the hierarchy of lovers is not a simple feat. All of us grew up being taught the gospel of husband-hunting: "It is just as easy to fall in love with a rich man as a poor one."

"Women come from a long tradition of measuring worth in monetary terms and status. It's embedded in our culture, especially with regard to men," says psychologist Carole Wade, coauthor of *The Longest War: Sex Differences in Perspective.* "That kind of thinking can keep women from even recognizing good men. But it's difficult to change. It calls for a radical transformation in values."

Barbara, a successful author, admits that before she could allow herself to be committed to a partnership with Richard, she had to struggle to overcome her old princess's training that she must marry a wealthy prince. Richard works in a copy shop and is not interested in pursuing a career; he is content to have a job. Barbara earns more than triple his salary and will earn proportionately even more than he in the future. But Barbara says she has found that being with a man who is not a workaholic has its advantages. "Because Richard isn't focused on a career, I get a lot of his attention and caring. He has helped me slow down and smell the roses. We go on hikes, camp out, and enjoy life. We have a wonderful relationship, and I've learned that paychecks are less important than love, respect, and companionship. What I wanted most was an egalitarian partnership, and we have that."

We women have a lot to gain by rethinking the old rule about who must be the provider. Even so, I'm not predicting that marriages between high-salaried women and low-salaried men will appear on next year's list of hottest trends. I do feel certain, though, that as women become more successful and well paid, relationships won't be so thrown off balance if a woman earns the higher income. I was expressing this wisdom to a woman I had just finished interviewing, when I noticed her eyes flashing. She responded by letting me know that she would never put up with a man who had trouble accepting her being more successful in business than he. "It makes me so furious to hear about how men are so leery of competent women. They ought to grow up," she exclaimed indignantly.

I understand her frustration. We certainly shouldn't have to put up with men's, or for that matter women's, archaic attitudes about women's place in the world. But waiting for the world to come to its senses has limited effectiveness. Until it catches up with us, we need to use rational thinking, not raw emotion, to get what we want. And this means we have to stop being so hesitant to enjoy our success and share equal power in our partnership. "Men are reluctant to give up power in a relationship, even to a partner earning more money. That makes sense," observes writer Linda Lehrer. "The British didn't give up the Thirteen Colonies because it was the fair or logical thing to do. It took a war to make them see the light. If you want a share of the power you have to ask for it. You may even have to fight for it. At least you have to believe you have a right to it." Read that paragraph again. Unless we take it to heart, we won't go much farther with equality than where we now stand.

7

MEN AND THE GREAT DUST BALL CAPER

> We used to be so happy! (Said when-
> ever it was his turn to do something.)
> Meaning: Life without housework is
> bliss. (No quarrel here. Perfect agree-
> ment.)
>
> —Patricia Mainardi,
> *The Politics of Housework*

There are any number of things that upset women about the lack of equality in their relationships—decision making, money, leisure time. But the one thing that drives us the craziest is housework. Almost every woman I interviewed—and I'm not exaggerating—is either annoyed, angered, or frustrated with her beloved because he isn't doing his fair share of maintaining their shared household.

Housework definitely is a lightning rod for family tension, and it isn't a light-weight issue. This constant battling over who does what household chores has serious consequences; it is one of the heaviest anchors holding down our high hopes for equality. Being stuck doing most of the grunt work around the house makes women so angry that they are unable to concentrate on solutions to the problem. Instead, we waste our energy denouncing the beastly nature of our partner. Yes, though at work we may be paragons of grace under pressure, we fall from grace at home: we nag, we argue, we bicker, bicker, bicker. Not only are these tactics totally ineffective, they lead to other, even more dramatic displays of disaffection, such as burnt meals, absolute silence, and sexual standoffs. Even divorce. After a speech I gave recently, a woman from the audience pulled me aside to tell me that she was considering leaving her husband because she was fed up with arguing with him to do more of the housework. She's not the only woman thinking divorce. I've heard that comment from women all over this country. I believe it's the "aha" factor—the connection between a woman's resentment of the "second shift" (putting in a full day at the office and then coming home and putting in another shift of housework) and her realizing she is tired of dealing with it, and him. This "aha" moment is why more women than men have considered divorce. Researchers Joan Huber and Glenna Spitze asked 1,360 husbands and wives if the thought of getting a divorce had ever crossed their minds. They found that more wives than husbands had thought about divorce, and that wives had thought about it more because of their resentment of having the lion's share of household tasks. Huber and Spitze also found that women whose husbands shared household tasks were less likely to contemplate divorce than women who had to shoulder all the domestic burden. And the more helpful the husband, the less often visions of divorce crossed the wife's mind. The researchers noted as well that for each daily household task that the husband performed at least half the time, the wife was about 3 percent less likely to have thoughts of divorce.

What can we learn from this?

If we are ever to have the kind of equal and happy relationship we want with the man we love, we have to find a way to resolve the serious problem of fairly sharing the work of running a home. Sharing household chores is directly related to the stability and happiness of a partnership. In her landmark book about this phenomenon, entitled *The Second Shift*, Arlie Hochschild describes the great payoff for both men and women who successfully resolve this conflict: "The happiest two-job marriages I saw during my research were ones in which men and women shared the housework and the parenting. What couples called good communication often meant that they were good at saying thanks to one another for small aspects of taking care of the family. Making it to the school play, helping a child read, cooking dinner in good spirit, remembering the grocery list, taking responsibility for cleaning up the bedrooms—these were the silver and gold of the marital exchange." Perhaps Hochschild's most valuable piece of wisdom for men to heed is this: "A wife will never tell her husband she wants a divorce while he is doing the dishes."

No responsible soul would suggest there is not real tension between the sexes, or that many women don't indeed have cause to view men with frustration. It's also true that we know most males are not ogres but are just trying to muddle through. So when the topic of housework comes up, it's best to keep in mind that your goal is not to prove your mate at fault, but to forge a bond with him so that the two of you are working together in a partnership.

One of the best ways to deal with these issues in your romantic relationship is to make better use of the skills you practice at the office to deal with difficult people and resolve thorny issues. However, no matter what strategies you use to aim for a partnership where the household chores are shared, there is a critical first step: you have to be sure you are communicating with someone who is listening, or you'll end up talking to yourself or the television screen.

GETTING HIS ATTENTION

Remember the one about the mule?

A man is walking down a road when he sees a farmer screaming at a mule who is sitting in the middle of the road.

"Hey," the man says, "Why are you yelling at this poor animal?"

"Because," the farmer answers, "I have to get home and this mule won't budge."

"Well, yelling at him won't get him to move," the man says. "You've got to talk to him. You've got to mesmerize him with your commands. Here, let me show you."

With that, the man picks up a big stick, walks up in front of the mule, and hits him over the head.

"What?" says the farmer, "I thought you were going to talk to him."

"I am," the man says. "But first I have to get his attention."

There have to be better jokes than that old saw, but there is no better reminder that in order to communicate with anyone, you must have his attention.

"Whether you're meeting with clients or employees or you're behind closed doors with a potential employer, you have a limited amount of time to make your point," explains Helayne Spivak, a creative executive at the Young & Rubicam ad agency. "In advertising this is relatively easy. You can rely on music, color, editing techniques, sound effects, and dozens of other devices." In real life we don't have the advantage of advertising's bells and whistles; we have to be very determined to get ourselves heard. "Back when I started in the business, I was in a meeting and had a point to make," recalls Spivak. "I started to speak. Someone talked over me. I started again. I must have started the same sentence five times and still wasn't able to get out enough syllables to make up a short word. Finally, I got up and started to walk out. I said, 'You're obviously not interested in what I have to say, so I'll come back when you are.' Suddenly everyone was interested. 'No, no, stay,' they said, and I got to speak, uninterrupted."

Sounds too dramatic? Maybe. But when it comes to communicating with men, sometimes it's hard to cut through.

WHY WE'RE STILL TALKING ABOUT WHO DOES THE DISHES

> Phil Donahue really is the greatest husband in the history of the Western world—and he's nothing to brag about.
>
> —Marlo Thomas

A man who loves his mate, cares about having a happy relationship, believes in equality between the genders, and is a thoughtful and sensitive person could never sit in front of the television set or stand idly by while his partner worked herself into a weary pile of bones. Right? Hardly! Most of us live with a man who, despite his vows of undying love for us, doesn't leap at the chance to relieve us of household tasks.

Many times during the course of writing this book, I walked through the kitchen on the way to my home office and found the previous night's dinner dishes, pots, and pans piled high in the sink. It baffled and infuriated me. Bob and I have a deal: I cook, and he does the dishes. But too often I cook, and he doesn't do the dishes (at least not right away). I mentally prepare the speech I'll deliver when he gets home. It'll have just the right touch of righteous anger; a full-blown logical discourse on the morality of keeping one's word; plus, of course, a sentence or two sharing how I feel when he does that. Yes. That should do it—make him see the error of his ways and repent. But wait. We've been down this path before, many times. It's a too-familiar script; I could play both of our parts. He'll defensively tell me that a deal is a deal and ours is that he will do the dishes, not when and not how. He'll go on about his right to do them when it is convenient for him. I'll retort that the deal is that he do the dishes before the next morning when I have to look at them. He'll retort. We'll get upset with each other's unreasonableness, then we'll make up and play the scene all over again in a few weeks.

One day when I was staring for the umpteenth time at those dishes, visions of one of my former employees came to mind. I instantly recalled how frustrated I was with her concept of "a deal is a deal." Marilyn was brought on board to handle a special project, one with defined goals to be met (it was a foundation-funded project) on a tight time line. At first things went fine. Then she began to get behind. I would get anxious. We would meet and review the schedule we had agreed upon. She would get upset, saying she felt that it wasn't important *when* she produced the work as long as she made the final deadline. Before things went from bad to worse I knew I had to take action. We sat down, and I asked her how we could better work together on the project. After we discussed several new approaches, we agreed that she would make monthly reports on her progress. I promised I wouldn't bother her in between. She kept her end of the deal and I kept mine, and the project was not only a great success, it was completed right on time.

Although I had never made the connection before, it dawned on me that there was a common thread between that situation at work and the one at home. In both places I was faced with a dispute over getting something done by two different standards. Still, as frustrated as I was with Marilyn, I didn't get angry with her.

In business situations, I keep a cool head and focus not on the personalities involved but on resolutions to problems. Why, I wondered, couldn't I do that at home? Instead, I lose it. I hate having to remind anyone to keep up their end of a bargain. I feel like howling to the moon, "Why doesn't he just do his fair share and be done with it?"

In order to find an answer to that provocative question, I went back to the management strategy "studying the client." We can't design a blueprint for change until we have a better grasp of the reasons men argue with us so doggedly about the chores of daily living.

Our first clue about our "client's" behavior comes from Jesse Barnard, the eminent sociologist, who believes men and women have two entirely different perceptions of their marriage. There is "his" marriage, and there is "her" marriage.

In this light, we can see that a big part of the never-ending battle over housework stems from the different perspectives men and women typically have on the subject. While he may see himself as purely egalitarian in his willingness to "help out around the house," she resents that sort of attitude because she knows it is what saddles her with the primary responsibility for getting the work done in the first place. Men (I'm not justifying the male point of view; I'm just the messenger) tend to see housework as a trivial issue, so commonplace and simple to do that it's hardly worth making a fuss over. Women, on the other hand, experience housework as a major burden on their shoulders—and one that weighs heavily along with all their other career and family responsibilities.

While men may agree intellectually that they ought to bear a fair share of this burden, it's emotionally very hard for them to get excited about a sink full of dishes or an unmade bed. They were never raised, as women were, to get ego gratification from the state of cleanliness of their home. Men simply can't stir up within themselves the righteous indignation women automatically feel at the sight of a messy living room. Women typically get embarrassed and apologize when a guest finds dust on the coffee table. Most men couldn't care less, because they don't notice a dust ball unless it grows large enough to obstruct their view of the television screen.

Other men harbor a motel mentality. Why bother getting into a sweat cleaning the house when the motel maid will be around to clean up? Another thorny issue arises when a man is willing to share housework but defines the tasks in a minimalist way. For example, one man I interviewed said, "When it's my turn to cook I get Kentucky Fried Chicken or buy deli sandwiches." Some men stock up on paper plates and microwave dinners. Others put the clothes in the washer, but not the dryer, or never put them away. If we comment, we are overzealous hausfraus. Maybe at times we *are* a little too fussy and it would be a good idea to negotiate a lesser standard of housekeeping. But I find that most women care less and less about the traditional white gloves good-housekeeping test. We are perfectly willing to go along with lumpy beds and clothes that aren't folded just so. What matters is that we aren't stuck doing all of the chores.

After you have analyzed the above information, you may arrive at this conclusion: when it comes to getting men to do an equal share of housework, forget about using strategies that rely on guilt over not pulling one's own weight or pride in one's work as motivation. Since men really, deep down, don't care much about spotless floors, it's hard for them to work up the incentive to get out the mop. It is simply a waste of our time and talent to expect men to take the initiative and do what has to be done, say, the way a highly motivated employee would. At least not until we have had an opportunity to change our past ineffective approaches and implement new, effective ones.

Men tend to be mystified that women attach so much importance to a clean house, and feel resentful when their mates seem more intent on getting the laundry done than on spending an enjoyable evening together. They just don't comprehend the basic principle that most women are incapable of relaxing as long as their home is dirty or chaotic.

Now that we've covered (albeit briefly) men's and women's perspectives on the curse of housework, let's move on to another part of our assignment to "study the client." Read through the following list, and see if any of these dynamics apply to your partner.

The way he feels about your role. Some men see cooking and cleaning as an expression of love from their wives. When his wife complains about the burden of homemaking, he may feel unloved.

The way he feels about your job. Men who resent their wives' ambitions sometimes see their wives as selfish for wanting a career instead of devoting themselves to housekeeping. Even if his wife's income is essential, a man may feel that her job has deprived him of a full-time wife. Men who support their wives' careers are far more likely to help shoulder the burden of housework.

The amount of housework he's expected to do. Many men are happy to "help out" their wives, but feel somehow less masculine if they actually have to take responsibility for what they have been taught is women's work.

The role structure of his parents' marriage. If his own mother had a job, or his father gladly tied on the apron strings, he'll probably make a much more willing domestic partner.

His childhood training. If he learned to help with household chores as a child, he won't feel it is unusual or unmanly to take some measure of responsibility for running the household.

Given all of the above, here's what we have to deal with. Husbands who are avoiding housework aren't necessarily selfish, unloving, or spoiled by their Mommys. They simply haven't yet adopted new gender roles that fit the needs of their families. Maddeningly, they seem to put more energy into developing strategies for getting out of family work than they put into doing household chores. Men want to be told what to do around the house. Not until a woman whispers the word "vacuum" in his ear, for instance, does he have a clue that the house needs vacuuming.

A problem women face over men's lack of ability to see above and beyond household dust and grime is that we don't want to supervise our spouses. It often seems easier for a woman to do something herself than to take on the role of training supervisor and explain the procedures to a grudging mate. As one woman complained, "Whatever happened to his passion for teamwork and all the stuff guys supposedly learn from sports?" Says another, "He's not even in the game. He doesn't make a move unless he gets orders from me, Mommy, the CEO of Home, Inc. It's my responsibility to find day care, call the school, keep track of homework, chart the workload, and get it done."

The most curious thing to me is how much men "imagine" they are helping around the house. Complained a man I interviewed, "She doesn't appreciate half of what I do—select our insurance, keep the car running, watch the bond market . . ." Another man told me that he "makes salads," and "maintains the plants." He was referring to indoor plants (I counted three pots, and one was a cactus); the couple lives in an apartment complex where the manager maintains the landscape. He wasn't trying to be witty; he was just listing for me the things he does to "help around the house." Men, of course, do contribute their labor to running the home. And many of their tasks are grubby and back breaking—cleaning the driveway or trimming the bushes.

The inequality of the burden on women is that the family work we do is unrelenting, repetitive, and routine—cleaning, cooking, shopping, child care, laundry, and straightening up. The family work that men usually do is infrequent, irregular, and nonroutine—taking out the weekly trash, mowing the lawn, changing the oil in the car, and repairing things around the house.

In one nationwide survey, couples were asked how they divide up specific household tasks. Despite all of the talk about the sexual revolution, task assignments look very unrevolutionary.

Women

Cooking meals	82%
Doing the dishes	79%
Doing the laundry	88%
Washing floors	85%
Vacuuming	78%
Grocery shopping	75%

Men

Household repairs	79%
Lawn work	74%
Decide on investments	64%
Buy insurance	63%
Open bank account	56%

[Source: "Great Sexpectations: The Attitudes of the Sexes." D'Aroy Masius, in *Working Mother,* September, 1992]

On a day-to-day basis, most men do so little in the way of housework that the research in this area could be called much ado about nothing. In one study of sex roles and housework, the researchers found that men actually contribute more to the *need* for household work than they contribute to its completion. It gives one pause, doesn't it?

The reasons women haven't won the housework battle, or even had a draw, are complicated. The essential question may not be who does what kind of household chores, but who has the power to get out of doing them. When I ask men at my seminars why they don't do more of the housework, I usually get the same kind of excuses we discussed earlier. But one day a man in Oklahoma City said something that clicked for me. He very matter-of-factly explained, "Men don't do housework because they don't have to." Click. Women, because of our socialization and our commitment to our family and the relationship, simply cannot refuse to do the chores. Men feel they have a choice and if they don't want to do it, they don't. In many cases, studies do show that the division of household labor is related to the man's stronger position of power—his higher earnings. High-income husbands do less household tasks than other groups of men. And it's not just because more of their tasks are hired out—they don't do their share of the tasks *not* hired out.

The reality here is that men, high-income or not, have the status quo in their favor. Sonya Rhodes states, "Many men—on some level—think that if they just refuse to help, either by saying no to your requests or not following through on their promises, they'll continue to get away with doing less." And their past experiences have proven to them that they do get away with it, usually with a minimal amount of retaliation.

Of course, not all fights over household chores are about power struggles. Some are about housework, plain and simple.

"Men have to adjust," claims Michael Kimmel, a spokesman for the National Organization for Changing Men. "Only 18 percent of families today have a breadwinning man and a stay-at-home mom. So if she's bringing in half the income, her man will have to do half the housework." Kimmel makes it sound easy. And it is, when the man has egalitarian attitudes; all he has to do is act on his beliefs. But if the man doesn't have those beliefs or doesn't act on them, what can the woman do?

STAND TALL AND CARRY A BIG LIST

Ken Druck, a psychologist in private practice in San Diego and coauthor of *The Secrets Men Keep*, doesn't mince words. "It should be very clear by now that no one can get her partner to feel or want anything he doesn't choose to feel. Men will only share the responsibility in a relationship when they decide that it is worth the investment."

Don't you mince words either. Be forthright: the house (and if you are parents, the children) belong to both of you, and since you work outside the home just as he does, he will have to carry his weight inside the home just as you do. So far, so good. But what if you get little or no response from him or a noncommittal nod of the head indicating he hears you—followed by no action? If he gets a glazed look in his eye the minute you broach the topic, don't be surprised, but don't be put off, either. Therapist Sonya Rhodes advises, "You can say, 'I have the feeling you think housework isn't important enough for you to spend time on it. I feel the same way. I know you value order and sanity as much as I do, so what do think we should do?' By taking this approach, you're defusing psychological warfare by striking an adult alliance with him. You're saying, 'We both hate housework, but we're in this together.'"

Once you've made this effort, take a deep breath. Now you have to assess whether he cares and wants to share, or if his lack of response reflects something besides inexperience and confusion. "There are men who are unreachable, who will respond by deflecting your concerns and avoiding confrontation," says Druck. "A woman who is with a man like that has to carefully weigh what she is getting from the relationship against what she is giving up for it, in order to decide if it is a relationship worth staying in."

That's a very sticky issue, but one you can't ignore. Let's take a positive approach and determine your partner is a man who is willing to negotiate a more equitable division of household tasks and is open to discussing how to go about it with you.

Be honest about how much you resent having to do more than your share. Be calm, but don't tiptoe around the blood and guts of the issue. Be concrete about the effect his not sharing has on you, particularly on your self-esteem and your energy level. Explain to him in graphic detail how his actions make you feel—depressed, unloved, foolish, trapped—whatever is accurate. The trick to this kind of confrontation is not to get hooked into an emotional tirade about his past negligence or slothfulness. It could be that your constant habit of doing the chores has given him the impression that deep down you really don't mind so much. And from the vantage of his easy chair, it can look as if you are making things out to be worse than they are. What's a few dishes, a little dust, some newspapers scattered on the floor between friends and lovers? The important thing is to convey to him that you are serious about expecting him to make a change. Drop dead, all grown-up, take no prisoners serious. Don't underestimate the power of being committed to what you want.

Druck suggests that you begin to define your position by organizing a list of ten things you want him to participate in. Keep reworking the list until it reflects exactly what you want from him. Then, make a list of ten things you no longer want to do. For some of us, this includes personal chores such as picking up socks or gathering coffee cups from here and yon. For others, the list might consist of more complex issues, such as having to be the couple's social secretary. Your list may be a combination of both. Choose *one* of the ten issues on your list as the item you will concentrate on. This list-making technique is the very same as putting together a flow chart at the office that delineates who will do what. The difference is that in our performance objectives at the office it wouldn't be politically bright to list what we *won't* do. In our personal relationship, though, we need to put it all down—the good, the bad, and the won't do—to lessen the chances of a misunderstanding about our goals. Keep this list handy, because as we discuss strategies for implementing changes in your relationship, you'll need to refer back to the priorities on it.

We know that we cannot *force* men to do more housework or take responsibility for doing it. We cannot demand their cooperation. Clearly, other approaches—reasoning, nagging, threatening—have not worked either. Therefore, the next step is to try something else. We can incorporate what we know about motivating and managing people into improving the balance of sharing responsibility for home chores.

REACH HIM, TEACH HIM

You simply cannot be too specific about what you want to see happen. Follow the advice of Bruce Younger, a New Jersey–based merchandise buyer. Younger negotiates with designers and manufacturers in the United States and abroad. "Make sure your request is structured so the other party can agree to it and then act on it. Break your requests down into steps: 'Can you give us the two hundred men's sport coats? Can you ship them by the fifteenth?' Go for a 'yes' on the first step, and second, and so on."

"People usually relate better to concrete rather than abstract thinking," suggests psychotherapist Muriel Prince Warren, who practices in New York. "Give him one solution he can act on and you're more likely to get what you want: 'Sweetheart, can you wash the dishes while I run to the store? Think about exactly what it is you want him to do. Don't just say, 'Cut up the celery.'"

I know, I know. It seems so obvious, so elementary. And it is, to you. But to him it may be the first time he has ever cut up celery. You will have to show him. Although little children scarcely two years old shout out the demand, "Me do it! Me do it myself!" it's unlikely your spouse will do the same.

Annoying as it is, we must accept the fact that our spouse may not have much in the way of housekeeping skills. His level of ineptitude may be appalling. Many men are conditioned to believe they are naturally poor housekeepers or just don't have the right chromosomes to master the tasks, just as women have been conditioned to view themselves as klutzes in sports or dunces about math. Be confident he does have the ability to perform household tasks. Patricia Mainardi, discussing the politics of housework, points out, "A man can cook if he does it on a hunting or a fishing trip; he can wield a skillful needle if he does it mending a tent or a fishing net; he can even feed and clean a toddler on a camping trip." But it seems men are only able to perform in selected sites. She adds, "Few of the skills of the homemaker are beyond his reach as long as they are practiced in a suitably male environment." Be clear with him that his amnesia about how to do these tasks when he is not on traditional male turf is not cute. You believe he already has terrific skills and what he lacks, you will teach him. Reassure him that you aren't expecting him to do things that will emasculate him. Remind him that most of the world's renowned chefs are men. And most of the most famous housekeepers are, well . . . quit while you're ahead.

This means that instead of berating your spouse for doing something poorly, play teacher—as much of a pain as that is. Of course, if he hasn't caught on after a few of these teaching sessions, he may be feigning ignorance and incompetence to get out of doing the chores. If that's the situation—the correct scientific term for his behavior is goldbricking—it is back to the drawing board.

Remember, while you can't control your spouse's behavior, you do have the power to control your own. You can't make him do his share, but you don't have to pick up his slack, either. Sooner or later the mess and the lack of clean clothes will make the statement loud and clear that it's time to discuss a plan of action.

Before you begin that discussion, think again of the tactics you use at the office. How would you motivate an employee? Would you talk about his or her job as one to be loathed, one that nobody wants to do? Of course not. You would look for the positive, upbeat side to the task. It's the same at home. "How can you expect to convince your husband to do his fair share of the household chores," asks Susan Moller Okin, a contributing editor for the *Utne Reader*, "if your attitude toward them is one of sheer repulsion? 'Honey, I think you should start spending at least fifteen hours a week doing excruciatingly dull and painful hard labor.' He'll feel like you've tried, convicted, and sentenced him to prison camp for some imagined sins, and he'll understandably begrudge your new attitude about equality. Don't try to make him feel guilty for responding naturally to the way he has been conditioned. A better attitude is to invite him in to the secret realm of homemaking and open doors that have previously been barred to him.

"Keep in mind," Okin continues, "when planning to divide up household work, that not all tasks are created equal. Don't just make a list of chores and divide it up. Take some time to analyze each task—noting the frequency with which it must be performed, the amount of time it takes to perform it, what skills are required, and if it must be performed at a specific time or with essential deadlines." This strategy is the basic job assessment review and is an excellent way to get a perspective on what household tasks involve. In fact, this technique of weighing different factors on the job to determine the exact ways a job is performed has become critical now that equal pay for equal work is a big issue in government and corporate America.

Okin also notes that it is important to divide up the more creative and pleasant tasks as well as the most dull and tedious ones. But keep your eye on the fine print. It is still an equity issue if he always buys himself out when it's his turn and she doesn't buy herself out when it's her turn. Or when he handles his end of the bargain by hiring out chores when the couple can't afford to have a maid or send the laundry out to be done.

"AUTOPSY" THE SITUATION

"You have to ask yourself if this is what you want to do with your life," advises Marietta, a partner in a Wall Street law firm. "Focusing on career takes a great deal out of you; it takes a lot of endurance to hang in there . . . I was poor for a long time before I got out of school, and I used to plan all the exciting things I'd do when I could finally afford to. Well, after I had the money, I didn't have the time. I thought about learning to speak Italian, for instance, and play the flute. The problem was that between trying to have a relationship with Jack, doing most of the home maintenance, and sometimes being at the office around the clock, I was running myself into the ground.

"Working this hard on my job is not my lifelong intention. It is what I have to do now. But in return for this nose-to-the-grindstone effort, I have the gratification of being part of a top law firm and doing first-rate work.

"At home, I felt my life was falling apart at the seams. I would be frantically trying to get a dinner on the table, and Paul would be watching the news on TV. It drove me up the wall. Finally, I 'autopsied' the situation and put together a plan of action. I presented my case in the same 'professional' manner I use in my practice. I straightforwardly told him I couldn't keep up the hours at the office, do all of the maintenance for the house, and feel very loving toward him. But I wasn't about to give up this great career opportunity, so other things had to change. I was surprised to find out that he thought I had become a 'workaholic' who enjoyed the overload.

"We put together an action plan. We decided that our long-range goals were for each of us to succeed in our careers, for us to be supportive of each other, and to have a happy marriage. A short-range goal was to get me off on the right track in my career. His career is stable (he teaches English at a college), and he isn't under any particular deadlines or pressures. For six months he would be responsible for the maintenance and I would put my energy into my job. I would do some minimal things (my own laundry, for instance) but he would be in charge of shopping, cooking, cleaning. Then, we would switch responsibility and he would be off-duty for six months to work on his book. After this year is up, we'll revise our plan to fit our situation as it is at that time. Now, even with all of the pressure, I have time to walk every morning and I feel a lot better. Paul and I even have dinner together more often. I feel we are happier than we have ever been because we are working together as a team."

A key strategy Marietta used to improve her relationship is the very same one businesses use to solve tough people problems, one based on the principles of communication and feedback: constructive criticism.

CRITICISM THAT WORKS

Criticizing can be tricky business. Ask any woman who has been called a bitch or a nag. But constructive criticism is a powerful strategy for resolving problems. According to management consultant Mary Lynne Heldmann, "Many managers avoid criticizing their employees because they don't want to rock the boat or fear that a criticized worker will react badly. Not true; criticism is a valuable tool for communication. If you are a manager who is reluctant to step forward with constructive feedback, you should bear in mind its worth." Heldmann points out that criticism doesn't create problems, it uncovers them. "Careful, thoughtful criticism prevents the buildup of uncomfortable, unhealthy feelings. Giving consistent, ongoing criticism is far better than allowing destructive feelings to accumulate and fester. If you procrastinate, you're more apt to thoughtlessly criticize in the heat of the moment, because your feelings have become too strong."

Here is a roundup of her suggestions for how to implement the technique of constructive criticism:

Describe the specific action and/or statement to your employee. Don't tell him what he doesn't do; stick to what he does do that bothers you. Don't use words like *always* or *never*. Be calm and nonjudgmental. Address only one behavior at a time.

Be low-key, not dramatic. You are negotiating a change in behavior, not trying to make him feel bad.

Think carefully about what the employee wants and what will motivate him, keeping in mind that people are more apt to be motivated by reward than by punishment.

Be careful not to use judgments and labels. Don't say "you're stupid/disorganized/wrong," etc. Judgment words reflect opinions; stick to the facts.

Every bit of Heldmann's advice on how to use criticism wisely at the office can be translated to our personal relationship with our mate. Now is the time to refer to that list Ken Druck recommended you put together. Meet with your mate and bring out the list, focusing on the number-one priority you selected. Then, using the technique of constructive criticism, work out a plan of action you and your spouse can agree upon. It's important to approach the discussion in the same calm, nonjudgmental way that you would if handling the same kind of situation at the office.

On the home front, offering constructive criticism without having it taken personally is one of the most effective ways to deal with touchy subjects such as control issues, sharing household tasks, and changing the status quo. Be warned, however, that as helpful as the technique of constructive criticism can be, it takes real skill to apply it.

Too often we justify an angry attack on our partner as *constructive* criticism, a strategy that fools no one. Criticizing our mate, no matter how lofty our intentions, can be more than tricky; it can be treacherous. No one likes to be criticized, and most of us hate having our flaws pointed out. "Making room for opinions other than our own is heroic work," asserts Nancy K. Austin, a Capitola, California–based management consultant. "Everyone knows that even a teeny complaint has a half-life of about fifty years for the person on the receiving end." (So that's why it takes so long to get over performance appraisals!) "Compliments, according to a similar law of physics, vaporize in thirty seconds flat."

"Good criticizing," as therapist Sonya Rhodes sees it, "means talking about your differences, and when clients ask me how to get started, I always say, 'Gently, very gently.'" She goes on to explain. "There's a good reason for this. When a spouse is critical, it may sound all our alarms because we're reminded of being disciplined by our parents. We may feel transported to a time when we were small and vulnerable. For that reason, use a tone appropriate to a peer-to-peer discussion—not the same voice used to scold the kids. Even when we're spoken to as adults, we may feel put down and demeaned, which are very primitive feelings." In other words, don't be surprised by your spouse's strong defensive responses to your well-intended criticism. Often our reactions to criticism have more to do with those childhood emotions than with what's happening in the here-and-now. You can avoid or at least minimize a negative reaction by thinking before you speak and monitoring your speech patterns.

At the risk of sounding overly optimistic, my advice is to treat criticism as feedback and the points of contention as a loving confrontation where both partners can count on feeling supported and cared for, not unloved and censured. Remember, go gently, very gently.

KNOW WHAT YOU WANT

Like Marietta, we each need to "autopsy" our own situation. If the burden of household maintenance is draining your time and energy, if it begins to jeopardize your career achievement plans, you have to examine your options. Whatever it is that is making your marriage suffer, you can't afford not to speak up about it. If you don't speak up, you may develop a core of painful resentment that will eventually erupt, and it won't be a pretty sight.

We can accomplish our goals a lot more quickly if we call on our sense of humor. You could do as the Greek wives once did to persuade their husbands to come around to their way of thinking—go on a sex strike. However, the flaw to this tactic is that it punishes the innocent as well as the guilty (you know who you are). We could consider journalist Debra Kent's suggestion and "offer an incentive." Kent elaborates, "If he's the kind of guy who's most inclined to give when he knows he'll get something back, let him know that your interest in sex is directly related to having energy, and feeling good about his contribution to the household. Tell him that when you have more time, more energy, and less resentment, he just may wind up with more and better sex." When I mentioned this little gem of a recommendation to a man I interviewed he seriously responded, "Hey, don't be too quick to throw that idea out. I think she is on to something that will work." If that idea reminds you too much of "working girls" or sounds too manipulative, skip it and go on to being TACTful.

THE TACT STRATEGY

I asked Jean, the vice president of a paper manufacturing plant, if housework was an issue in her marriage. (I especially wanted to hear her views because a mutual acquaintance had told me that Jean is a strong, independent woman with, apparently, a very successful marital partnership.) She nodded her head yes, then shook it in the negative. "It used to be a bigger problem than it is now. We are making progress." She went on to explain. "Raul is a sloppy person and I'm neat. It would drive me to distraction to see his stuff littered all through the house—layers of coats over a chair, stacks of books and papers everywhere, masses of dirty clothes on the floor. We don't have to clean our house; I have a professional cleaning service. So that wasn't the problem; the problem was keeping the house tidy. He'd say I was too picky and bossy, and I'd argue that he was inconsiderate.

"One day a friend, Alice, came to pick me up to go to a concert. As she walked in the door I explained that all the stuff piled up belonged to Raul. I began to apologize when she cut me off. She laughingly suggested I henceforth dub them 'Raul's Piles' and sell tickets to auction them off. Or, she smiled, I could put them on the tourist tours of Albuquerque (See the Piles of Raul, Astonishing Troves of Treasures!). She simply broke me up. And put me on the right track. I had been so upset with his behavior, I hadn't seen any humor in it or any way to turn things around.

"At the office, I'm not so grumpy. Humor comes second nature to me as a way to smooth over rough spots, especially since I work in a blue-collar industry and many men are still uneasy about a Lady Boss. And I learned long ago that if you order someone to do something in an angry tone they respond badly. They may do it, but they will resent you and eventually this will sour your relationship. Better to use a little humor to sweeten the pot.

"Another administrative technique of mine is to break down a big job into manageable components. So I set my sights on the goal of having him pick up something every day without either of us getting mad at each other.

"The next day, when we both arrived home for work, I offered him a challenge. We would flip a coin to determine who had the honor of picking up and putting away one of his famous piles. Or I'd arm wrestle or race him around the park for the privilege. He good-naturedly said he got my point (he even smiled at Alice's little name for his stacks of stuff) and said he would take care of it. And he did. Just one pile. And that was it.

"At the end of the week, it was clear that I had to try something else. I've never consciously used my management style at home, but it suddenly occurred to me, why not? When we sat down to talk, I went with the same approach I use at the office to discuss a problem over an employee's job performance. It's called the TACT system: Tell, Affect, Change, and Trade-off."

TACT works like this:

Tell. Talk about the other person's behavior.

Affect. Describe how the behavior affects you or the organization.

Change. What has to change? (Jean put their problem in the category of how to constructively give each other feedback about what they could do differently.)

Trade-off. State the positive consequences of a change in behavior.

Jean continues, "Instead of resorting to threats and counterthreats, this time we stuck to the topic of how we could all live happily together in the same house—me, Raul, and Raul's Piles. So we worked out a compromise. He can pile things up all he wants in our guest bedroom, the only stipulation being that when we have guests he would somehow put all of his treasures out of sight. Raul gave up using the whole house, and I gave up having every room in the house look picture perfect.

"At work I accept that some employees are neater and more conscientious about their work space than others. At home, I've had to come to terms with the fact that my marriage partner is—well—a slob. I also have to listen to his point of view, which is that he thinks I am a neataholic and overly self-conscious about the way the house looks. It isn't an easy compromise, but we like each other again!"

Jean reviews for me how she applied the principles of TACT:

"I was very specific about what behavior I wanted to discuss.

"I expressed to him that I found his behavior very uncaring and disrespectful of my right to live in a comfortable environment.

"We discussed what each of us could do to deal with the situation, and we each talked about what we could do to change the things that disturbed the other.

"I stated the positive consequences of a trade-off. By getting a handle on the clutter, it would be a lot more pleasant around the house because we wouldn't be constantly on edge with each other, and solving the issue would improve our relationship."

The key to Jean's successful approach was her lighthearted tone. A woman who attended my seminar and who handles peer reviews suggested that things go smoother when the parties involved are relaxed. Maybe push the limits a little—wear a mask (the wicked witch of the north, Miss Piggy, or whatever strikes your fancy) to the bargaining table. Naturally, a lot would depend upon your office culture (your colleagues might not be amused), and as for the home culture—lighten up.

WHEN ALL ELSE FAILS

There are times when all the advice you get falls flat. Other people's experience doesn't relate to your situation, the expert's insight doesn't click, and your friends' advice proves useless. Action is definitely called for. But what action?

Helayne Spivak again offers us inspiration, this time through the example of a friend who had recently been promoted to the position of account executive. With the territory came an art director who was an advertising legend. This guy, Spivak recalls, only cared about creating great and meticulously crafted advertising and "he ate young account executives not just for breakfast but for lunch and dinner as well.

"Only too aware of all this, but determined to deal with him anyway, she knocked on his open door one day. No response. She walked into his office. He didn't look up. She said hello and introduced herself. He didn't look up. She stood, silent, for a minute or so. He still didn't look up.

"Finally, acting on an impulse she still can't explain, she went over to his couch, where all of his precious ads were neatly laid out, and with one arm swept them onto the floor and settled in on the couch to wait. He looked up. He said hello. And they worked together peacefully and respectfully for ten years after that."

The point is, if you want to change your partner's behavior, the most important place to begin is by changing your own. Over time, couples tend to establish patterns of relating to each other in which one partner's specific action automatically triggers a particular response in the other. The second partner's response then causes an automatic reaction from the first, thus setting off a chain of reactions that becomes an entrenched form of communication. Usually, neither partner realizes how his or her actions are affecting the other, so it is very hard to know what is really going on between you.

When you feel you have already been specific about your feelings and desires, with minimal results, your spouse's negative reaction (or lack of reaction) may have less to do with the actual nature of your request than with the way you've been communicating it. Maybe you've been on automatic and aren't getting through to each other. It brings us back to the story of the mule—letting your spouse know that you really are determined to shake up the status quo in your relationship means getting his attention.

Remember my anguished arguments with my partner about the dirty-dishes "deal" we had struck? After one very long two-day siege of looking at dirty pots and pans, something within me just unwound. While Bob was watching the MacNeil-Lehrer report on television, I went out to the garage and got a garbage bag. I returned to the kitchen and loudly proceeded to put the pots and pans into the bag. I danced into the den and calmly asked Bob for his car keys. I told him I no longer was going to nag him about cleaning up the kitchen. From then on I would put any dirty pans that have been held hostage for more than twenty-four hours into a garbage bag and stow them in the trunk of his car. Whenever he felt the muse calling he could wash them. Or he could sell them, donate them, or throw them out. Whatever. He was shocked. Then he nearly fell off the sofa laughing. It was contagious, and I had to laugh myself. At any rate, he came around and reevaluated his end of the "deal."

My point? Even when it flies in the face of logic, sometimes you just have to follow your heart and do something differently— maybe even something outrageous!

THE JOURNEY: FROM WOMAN TO WOMEN

Underscoring everything I've said in this book is that the most effective way for a woman to negotiate an equal partnership at home is for her to bring her on-the-job competence to the bargaining table. Now I want to add another dimension to our understanding about becoming an equal partner with the man we love. Our relationship doesn't exist in isolation. Our efforts to have an equal partnership with our mate inside the four walls of our home are handicapped by the lack of equality between women and men in the world outside.

The most obvious barrier between women and the upper echelons of money and status in the workplace is, of course, the glass ceiling, the subtle old-boy bias that keeps women stuck at the threshold of the executive suite. We've heard it all before—men aren't comfortable with women because women don't fit in; we're not at ease with the jargon of sports and the military; we don't play golf; and we can't take a joke.

SHATTERING THE GLASS CEILING

Yes, we are working; over 45 percent of the work force is female. And every year a few more of us become managers, vice presidents, and directors of corporations. But while our cup isn't half empty, it's not exactly overflowing. In the early seventies, 99 percent of top management was male. Now, after years of affirmative action, 97 percent of top management is still—take a guess. Despite years of rosy predictions that once women put on their power pumps they would quickly ascend the corporate ladder, where do you find us? Packing the corporate pyramid base in staff positions, just as we have for decades.

How bleak is this picture? Women earn only 71 cents for every dollar the average man earns. The median annual salary for women ages 40 to 44 is now about $22,000 for full-time work. According to the Institute for Women's Policy Research, that salary is about the same as a 25- to 29-year-old man starting out in his career. Most women aren't even close enough to a glass ceiling to see it. In every workplace arena, from power to paychecks, women still lag behind men.

Clearly, our work is cut out for us. To have equality in our intimate partnership and in our public life, we must put energy into changing the fundamental roots of inequality that pervade every nook and cranny of society—social, cultural, commercial, and political. But despite the personal nature of each woman's journey, we won't get anywhere marching single file. We'll make the quickest progress if we go forward joining hands to form a strong political action group, a nineties sisterhood that will give us the clout we need to level the playing field.

Then we can use our united muscle to press for fundamental changes in a system that makes it difficult for a woman to balance a family life and a career, a system that fails to reward women with the same material compensation it gives men. We have to set our sights on fundamental change because change that is merely superficial leaves the underlying system intact. You can't get rid of sex discrimination in hiring, for example, simply through superficial changes like eliminating the "Help Wanted/Male" and "Help Wanted/Female" listings in the newspaper. You have to change the way interviewers and employers assess the candidates' qualifications by eliminating stereotypical gender-role thinking.

What's the direct connection between our collective political action and our quest for a more equal intimate partnership? Simply this: it's a symbiotic relationship—equality at home is connected to equality in the workplace, and vice versa. As the feminist movement taught us, the political is personal, the personal is political. We will negotiate from a stronger position at home when we have power and equal status to men in all other aspects of our lives.

WHEN WOMEN MAKE THE RULES

Many of our friends and coworkers are balancing motherhood and work, and whether or not we are mothers we need to put up a united front to compel the corporate world to accommodate women who are. Some women are well into their careers before they have a child. Others become mothers at the beginning of a career or before they enter the work force. Many women have babies right out of college, while others wait until just before their biological clock appears to be running out. Other women opt not to become mothers. Regardless of the choices women make about motherhood, we share a common bond of sisterhood.

Sharing information among ourselves is an absolute necessity. How many women are aware that the United States lags far behind other advanced, industrialized countries that have sophisticated systems to support working women's families? Consider this: French parents send their kids to nursery school for free. Most European women receive almost full pay while on maternity leave. Why are we so far behind such progressive policies? Because we don't have enough women sitting at the power-broker table, making sure that laws and policies in the workplace and government are based on female experiences and needs, not just those of males.

The most effective way for women to have an impact on a system that doesn't support working women is for women to put child care, paid parental leave, equal pay, and flextime—the bread-and-butter issues for women in the workplace—on the agenda. If we want our fair share of power and paychecks, women have to be in on making the rules and calling the shots in the governmental decision-making process. For the record, according to Rutgers University Center for American Women and Politics, even the few women who have gained a voice in government have made a critical difference. Women can now obtain credit in their own name, from credit cards to business loans, thanks to women in Congress who championed laws to insure that females have the same access to credit that males enjoy. Female legislators also helped push through the pregnancy-discrimination and equal-pay laws now on the books, and are sure to address other difficulties women face, including the need for family leave, funds for child care, and inequalities in the Social Security system.

WHAT WOULD A REASONABLE WOMAN DO?

The reason equality with men in both our public and private lives is not quite a reality yet is not that the women's movement has gone too far, as some social history revisionists are fond of saying. We haven't gone far enough. One of my favorite quotes concerning the futility of moderation was uttered by Julia Sugarbaker of TV's "Designing Women": "All you find in the middle of the road is a yellow strip and a dead possum."

Judging by a recent *Business Week* survey of four hundred female managers, a number of women executives agree with Ms. Sugarbaker—the middle of the road has little to offer us. A vast majority of these corporate and business women say they are losing their patience over the slow pace of equity in the workplace and are tired of stewing about it in silence. They urge women to form in-house caucuses, complain loudly and publicly about inequities, take legal action if they see evidence of discrimination, and generally challenge the old-boy-network rules.

Organized adversarial tactics are beginning to pay off. According to California State Treasurer Kathleen Brown, a company can't even compete for a piece of the state's billion-dollar Public Employees Retirement Fund unless that company's investment management team includes a woman. Likewise, the U.S. Department of Labor has responded to pressure from women's groups and announced it is determined to eradicate workplace prejudices against women.

The woman's point of view is also gaining clout in legal circles. Historically, courts relied on the "reasonable man" standard to decide cases; that is, a judge or jury used what a reasonable man would make of the facts of the case as the standard. But that measure didn't work in all situations for women. A man isn't likely to understand what it feels like to be a woman in an office where men make lewd comments or torment her with bullying tactics. But last year a circuit court made a major breakthrough by ruling that incidents of sexual harassment must be judged on the basis of whether a "reasonable woman" would find the acts offensive, intimidating, or hostile.

We are making progress. I think about the November 12, 1991, gathering of men and women marching to "Mobilize for Women's Lives" in Washington, D.C. In this milestone event, I proudly marched with the Planned Parenthood contingent from Atlanta (as an honorary "Georgia Peach for Choice") up Pennsylvania

Avenue to the steps of the U.S. Congress. A group of enthusiastic college students passed us chanting a rousing cadence:

We're feminists, we're pissed, and we're not going shopping.
What do we want?
Freedom!
When do we want it?
Now!

My colleague Kay Scott gave me a sideways challenging look, and we jumped right in without missing a beat, adding our voices to the those of the other reasonable women with renewed enthusiasm for the cause.

But before we get lured into thinking the demise of inequality is just around the corner, remember that male and female stereotyped gender roles, though not natural, seem natural to many people. To speed the progress toward equality, it's now time for men take on their fair share of the responsibility for dismantling the discriminatory barriers of stereotypical thinking about women. What can men do? They can insist that the Bluebirds among them start doing their homework.

THE EDUCATION OF THE BLUEBIRDS

The reasons men are not comfortable with women as equals has been traced to history, religion, and economics. And let's not forget the most commonly cited perpetrator of men's problems with women: their mothers. I believe, however, that there is another perfectly plausible explanation.

It all goes back to the first grade when children were separated into reading groups. To avoid the cruelty of labeling the slow readers as such, the groups were given names such as "Bluebirds, "Redbirds," and "Robins." Of course everyone soon knew that the Bluebirds were the slow group, and as the majority of this group were boys, the teachers enlisted the bright girls in the Robins and Redbirds to take part in an undercover plot to save the boys' egos. The girls were cautioned not to flaunt their superior reading ability and encouraged to help the Bluebirds feel good about themselves. Thus, the Robins and the Redbirds coyly covered up their true abilities while fussing over the Bluebirds on the playground and flattering them in the classroom. No one could have imagined that this sweet little ploy would eventually backfire on the very people who tried so hard to help—the girls. As the object of all of this fuss and favoritism, the Bluebirds learned to feel *very* good about themselves. So good, it was a short step to the Bluebirds' believing it was their duty, if not divine right, to rule all of the female birds. Now the grown-up Bluebirds sit at the helm of the boardrooms all over America, while the bright girls are still expected to flutter and flatter modestly from their positions as support staff or associate something-or-other.

The problem is that the Bluebirds never learned to read, and therefore are not able to read the handwriting on the wall: the Robins and the Redbirds are fed up with playing the old passive, demeaning cover-up games.

I see a way out of this mess. A sensible remedy to the problem is for men who lead corporations and government to educate the male Bluebirds among them about the negative nuances that sexism in the workplace propagates and how, in fact, sexism nibbles away the goodwill between men and women in every arena, including home.

Education programs to eliminate sexual harassment are now provided (in fact, required) by most large employers. But most of these programs slide over the root causes of sexual harassment—the lingering residue of patriarchy. As a result, those efforts don't do much to raise men's consciousness. Think about it this way: every day, at the office and at home, men face myriad conflicts and misunderstandings over their roles and responsibilities in this changing dual-wage-earning world. Even the most supportive of men are a bit at sea about how to deal with women as equals, colleagues, and friends, as well as lovers and mates.

What makes this situation more difficult—and loaded with emotional dynamite—is that when barriers to equality are discussed and women point to the glass ceiling, many men feel they are being personally, and unfairly, attacked. But based on the comments of men at my seminars, I've realized that there is a way to get beyond this impasse. When the causes and consequences of discrimination are handled in a direct, pragmatic, problem-solving manner—especially in the atmosphere of an adult educational workshop or a seminar—men don't knee-jerk defensively. In this setting, I've seen men come around to identify with sexism's basic unfairness to both genders and then become much more tuned in to women's feelings about the issue. Men hear, sometimes for the first time, that sexism harms not just some vague group of women but their moms, sisters, lovers, wives, and daughters, as well as the women they personally respect as colleagues. Once this "click" happens, they are more open to looking at how to resolve the problem at work, and this openness extends to their intimate relationships. Ah yes, the political is personal.

Which brings us back to that man you love and live with. How does he figure in this "sisterhood thing?" By advocating that women band together I'm not implying that men be left out. No male bashing here. Just the opposite. Every woman I interviewed longs for a world where men and women are allies, not adversaries. Men are, after all, the other half of the male-female equation. As members of the human species, we all harbor the same fears, wants, and needs. We are all afraid of rejection and alienation and try to avoid humiliation and failure. We all want to be loved, respected, and successful.

It's time the Battle of the Sexes is declared a truce.

THE DAYS OF *OUR* LIVES

It was 1970 when Gloria Steinem and Flo Kennedy came to Albuquerque for a NOW recruitment meeting on the campus of the University of New Mexico. (About 40 women showed up, including me in my bell bottoms.) Afterward, we retreated to someone's house to drink red jug wine, sit on the floor, and talk about politics and women's lives. I remember it vividly because it was the first time I had given serious thought to how women fared in this world compared to men. Although most of us were unaware of it at the time, we were on the cusp of a revolution—shortly to be identified as the women's movement.

In 1970, about half of all women between twenty-five and fifty-four had jobs; today it's over 75 percent—an overwhelming majority. Having our own income goes to the heart of profound changes in the way women perceive the world now and the way our world is starting to perceive us. The days when many women lived their lives as homemakers cloistered in the cozy confines of suburbia are, like the Old South, gone with the wind. Drive along a highway and PEOPLE AT WORK signs remind us that what started as a dramatic shift in women's expectations about their place in the world has altered the profile of the workplace.

Women's hard-fought right to choose a full life—to have both a loving home life and a productive and successful career, to be a mother or not, to have the freedom to make our own mistakes, to compete in sports and politics—has forever changed the way we live our lives.

We can expect even greater changes ahead as we journey over the bumpy, less-traveled roads toward equal partnership with the man we love. And all of us, men and women alike, are richer for it.

ENDNOTES

INTRODUCTION: LOVE'S GLASS CEILING

The term *dual career* was originated by R. Rapoport and R. Rapoport (1971) as one in which both spouses engage in work having a developmental sequence requiring a high degree of commitment and have roughly equal education, job status, and income. See *Dual-Career Families* (Harmondsworth, England: Penguin, 1971).

CHAPTER ONE: DO I HAVE TO GIVE UP MY CAREER TO BE LOVED BY YOU?

Page 7:
". . . if a wife's job interferes . . ." Philip Blumstein and Pepper Schwartz, *American Couples: Money, Work, Sex* (New York: William Morrow & Co., 1983).

Page 8:
[Even women with strong independent goals can be] "trapped between two sets of ideals." Dr. Gaylin's comments were quoted by Erica Abeel in her article entitled "Dark Secrets," *Esquire,* June 1984, p. 264. This classic article is still profound and relevant.

Page 9:
"Women have had such a long, distinguished career as caretakers . . ." In the above-cited *Esquire* article, psychologist Erica Abeel analyzes how the history of women as care-givers and in family support roles continues to impact today on the tendency of women to consider marriage and commitment as a possible trap. Also in the article, Dr. Abeel offers Dr. Ethal Person's theory that fear of loss of autonomy causes some women to postpone marriage.

Page 11:
"Whether they are professional or blue-collar . . ." Susan Faludi, *Backlash: The Undeclared War Against American Women* (New York: Crown Publishers, Inc., 1991). This is the most profound book on women's lives and sexism in decades. It is a *must* read.

". . . to keep daily 'stress diaries.'" Sociologists Elaine Wethington of Cornell University and Ronald Kessler of the University of Michigan compared stress experienced by men and women on the basis of information collected from "stress diaries" kept by the subjects. This study was reported in Rosalind C.

Barnett and Caryl Rivers, "The Myth of the Miserable Working Woman," *Working Woman*, February 1992, p. 64.

"Having a career even pays off in lower cholesterol levels!" These findings, of a study at the University of California at San Diego, were reported in "Health and Fitness Notes," *Vogue*, May 1992, p. 85.

Page 12:

"Not working would create more strains . . ." Survey results reported in Nancy Marshall, "Who Are the Happiest New Mothers?" *Working Mother*, May 1992.

Pages 12–13:

"In a study of 442 working mothers . . ." The research findings of Jeanne Bodin and Bonnie Mitelman were cited in "More Women Juggling Job, Family, Home," *Albuquerque Journal*, Sunday, May 22, 1983. See also "A Woman's Place," in Lois Blake, "The Stress of Staying Home," *Psychology Today*, July/August 1989. More recently see Marshall, *op. cit.*

Page 13:

Studies conducted by Rosalind C. Barnett at the Wellesley College Center for Research on Women focused on how women are affected by leaving the work force or reducing hours of work to return to homemaking. These findings were reported in Barnett and Rivers, "The Myth of the Miserable Working Woman," *Working Woman*, February 1992, p. 64.

"The Wellesley researchers found that women who work twenty hours a week or less . . ." *Ibid.*

"Most part-timers wind up more stressed out . . ." Not only do women who work part-time experience more stress than those working full-time, they lose out financially in the long run as well. "A new study shows that women who took time off from work—even only 6 months—were still making less than their peers 20 years later. The 2,000 women who took part in the study had one or two work interruptions, with a median gap of between 4 and 5 years. Researchers Joyce Jacobsen of Rhodes College in Memphis and Laurence Levin of Santa Clara University in California found that even short gaps hurt: More than a quarter of the women took off a year or less and never regained parity." Research findings quoted in "No Stay, No Pay," *Working Woman*, April 1992.

Page 14:

"There are two ways to look at women and work . . ." Barnett and Rivers, *op cit.*

"The more roles women have, the better off they are . . ." This quote by psychologist Virginia O'Leary was found in the *Self* magazine survey report entitled "Profile of Women Today," September 1989, p. 165. Confirming this finding are the recent studies conducted at Wellesley. Rosalind C. Barnett and her coauthors noted in the April 1992 issue of *The Journal of Personality and Social Psychology* that "the more roles a woman occupies, the better her mental and physical health." Barnett's current studies add support to earlier research findings, such as those reported by demographer Lois Verbrugge at the University of Michigan. Verbrugge noted that "not being involved leads to

196

depression." Her research was reported in Holly Hall, "A Woman's Place," *Psychology Today,* July 1989, p. 28.

Page 15:
"Don't let anybody kid you . . ." from Betty Friedan, "Where Do We Go From Here?" *Working Woman,* November 1986, p. 152.

Page 16:
"Whether delivered in fiery broadsides . . ." Susan Faludi, *op cit.* The backlash is a significant factor in women's lives, but it is not the only reason for inequities. Not only does the position of males depend upon social and economic class, but males also share with certain women whatever gain or loss they experience as members of high or low ethnic groups or classes. One of the shortcomings of any theory about male power and status is the tendency to ignore the reality that the position of men differs by ethnic group and social economic class. Men, like women, are not a collective group but a social segment within the society. William Goode, in "Why Men Resist," *Rethinking the Family: Some Feminist Questions.* Edited by Barrie Thorne and Marilyn Yalom (New York: Longman, Inc., 1982) points out that "in fact, one can observe that the position of women varies a good deal by class, by society, and over time, and no one has succeeded in proving that those variations are the simple result of men's exploitation." A very important book that examines male and female status and power is Warren Farrell's *The Myth of Male Power* (New York: Simon & Schuster, 1993). But Faludi makes an excellent case for the existence of the backlash phenomenon, especially when she backs up her observation that the messages did "manage to infiltrate the thoughts of women, broadcasting on these private channels its sound waves of shame and reproach."

"Working women tell themselves that if only . . ." Therapist Jo Ann Larsen's theory of "if only" rationalization on the part of women was cited by Dianne Hales, "Letting Go of Guilt," *Working Mother,* September 1992, p. 47.

Pages 16–17:
". . . more than 75 percent of women in advertising and related fields . . ." These findings were taken from the study report entitled "Women in Advertising Say Both Career, Family Possible," *Business Outlook,* July 21, 1986, p. 38.

Page 17
"My mother was convinced . . ." *Good Housekeeping,* October 1990.

"We have never rid ourselves of the fifties propaganda . . ." Rosalind C. Barnett and Caryl Rivers, "The Myth of the Miserable Working Woman," *Working Woman,* February 1992, p. 64.

Page 18:
"There is nothing wrong with *Martha Stewart Living* . . ." Betty Friedan's comments were taken from her article, "The Dangers of the New Feminine Mystique," *McCall's,* November 1991, p. 80.

Page 20:
Robert Bly, *Iron John* (Reading, Mass.: Addison-Wesley, 1990).

Sam Keen, *Fire in the Belly* (New York: Bantam Books, 1991).

Warren Farrell, *Why Men Are the Way They Are* (New York: McGraw-Hill, 1986).

Page 21:

"When my wife began her career . . ." W. W. Meade, "Changing Men, Changing Marriage," *Working Woman,* November 1986, pp. 171–172.)

"The increase in distress among men . . ." The comprehensive research study of men's mental health was conducted by Ronald Kessler and James McRae, Jr., at the University of Michigan's Institute for Social Research. The researchers also pointed out that "unfortunately, men's discomfort about not being the primary breadwinner can be further exacerbated by that other well-established threat to mental health: loss of economic status. Millions of traditional 'male' jobs that once yielded a living wage are evaporating in a recession and a restructuring global economy. Many men (and women) are caught in a difficult position of seeing their traditional position as the protector of women disappear and believe that a husband who cannot support his family is a failure as a man."

Kessler and McRae's findings were reported by Zick Rubin, "Are Working Wives Hazardous to Their Husbands' Mental Health?" *Psychology Today,* May 1988.

Page 22:

"Today more and more men . . ." Anthony Astrachan, *How Men Feel: Their Response to Women's Demands for Equality and Power* (New York: Anchor Press/Doubleday, 1986), p. 219.

"If he has more power at work . . ." Cher Thomas, California State University at Irvine, quoted by Marilyn Elias in "Two-Job Couples: Let the Man Rule," *USA Today,* June 19, 1991.

Page 23:

"Often the actual physical facts . . ." Ann Swanke, New School for Social Research, from Madeline Prober, "The Dynamics of Drive," *Glamour,* April 1990.

Pages 26–27:

"Somehow, without ever talking about it . . ." The experience of Susan, an educational consultant, was described by Jane Howard, "Lessons," *Lear's,* March 1990, p. 167.

Page 27:

"I don't want someone to be Mrs. Robert Sellers . . ." quoted from "What Do Black Men Really Want In a Woman?" *Ebony,* June 1992, p. 40.

Page 30:

"We speak to our parents differently . . ." quoted from Adele Scheele, "Pigeonholed: How to Break Out," *Working Woman,* October 1991, p. 46.

Page 31:

"Speak clearly, without hidden meaning . . ." Paula Ancona, "Here Are Tips for Dual-Career Couples," *Albuquerque Tribune,* September 12, 1991.

Page 32:
"I can't imagine my life without my children . . ." Barbara Berg, *The Crises of the Working Mother*. Quoted by Margaret Shakespeare, "The Career, the Husband, the Kids and Everything," *Working Woman*, December 1990, pp. 94–98)

Page 33:
Peggy's story about using her job skills at home from an article by Tamara Eberlein, "What I Learned at Home, What I Learned at the Office," *Redbook*, October 1991.

CHAPTER TWO: THE PARTNERSHIP

Page 36:
"Passion gets people into bed . . ." quoted from Michael Korda, "Partnership," *Self*, February 1982, p. 69. This article is more than a decade old, but he is so on-target it is as if he were writing today. I am in debt to him because his article is one of the seminal pieces that influenced my own thinking about the meaning of partnership.

Page 37:
"Partnerships tend to be alike . . ." Dr. David Hopkinson is quoted by Teresa Byrne-Dodge, "Partners: In Business, In Marriage," *American Way*, May 14, 1985, p. 34.

Page 38:
Johnnetta Cole quoted by Jill Soloman, "When Jobs Clash," *Time*, September 3, 1990, p. 84.

"[It] does not demand that the man . . ." quoted from Sol Gordon, *Why Love Is Not Enough* (Holbrook, Mass.: Bob Adams, Inc., 1988), p. 65.

Another view is that of sociologists John Altrocci and Ross D. Crosby (1989) who say that most of us have a mind-set about traditional and egalitarian marriages. When someone mentions a *traditional* marriage, we get an instant mental picture of rigid sex roles: a working husband and a homemaking wife, with Dad as the final authority in family conflicts. The words *egalitarian marriage* stir up visions of openness in communication, more flexible gender roles, and a conception that for marriages to be successful they need to be "worked on."

While the classification of couples into traditional and egalitarian camps can be useful as a shorthand way to describe the ways in which marriages are structured, it's not without its flaws. Just the words themselves—*traditional* and *egalitarian*—have some drawbacks: Each term has positive value connotations to some people and negative connotations to others. Thus we can't assume we are thinking the same thing when we refer to either of those terms.

Those terms can lead us to believe we have a good idea about how couples relate to each other depending upon the structure of their marriage. But we could be off base. Despite our notions of traditional marriages as entombed in sex-role stereotypes, studies have found that there are marriages which are self-described as traditional where the couple acts nontraditionally. Husbands and wives both provide emotional support, adapt, cooperate, and communicate with each other, although these have been seen as traditionally female tasks. For further information, I refer you to the article by Altrocchi and Crosby, "Clarifying and Measuring the Concept of Traditional vs. Egalitarian Roles in Marriage," *Sex Roles*, vol. 20, nos. 11/12, 1989.

"Both partners do the emotional and physical 'chores'. . ." from Sonya Rhodes and Marlin Potash, *Cold Feet: Why Men Don't Commit* (Psychology Book Club brochure, April 1988), pp. 9–10.

Page 42:
"Women were raised to believe . . ." Quoted from Maureen Dowd, "Power: Are Women Afraid of It or Beyond It?" *Working Woman*, November 1991.

"The key to influencing others . . ." in Linda Hill, "Under the Influence: Making Peers See Things Your Way," *Working Woman*, September 1991, p. 28.

Page 43:
"A classic power struggle involves two people . . ." from Susan Campbell, *Beyond the Power Struggle: Dealing with Conflict in Love and Work* (California: Impact Publishers, 1984), p. 23.

"Power is always an underlying factor in a marriage . . ." The quotation from Marie Richmond-Abbott's book, *Masculine and Feminine*, was taken from Anthony Brandt, "The Partnership," *Esquire*, June 1984, p. 227. This article is worth looking up—Brandt is very insightful.

"They organized their landmark study around . . ." Philip Blumstein and Pepper Schwartz, *American Couples* (New York: William Morrow & Co., 1983).

Page 44:
"Traditionally, men exercise a formal, authoritarian . . ." Ollie Pocs, *Our Intimate Relationships: Marriage and the Family* (New York: Harper & Row, 1989), p. 173.

"Studies and interviews with top executives . . ." Quoted in Dowd, *op cit.*, p. 99.

Page 46:
The analysis of decision-making styles (consensus model and executive model) were described by Teresa Byrne-Dodge in her article in *American Way, op. cit.*

Pages 48–49:
Stories of two couples quoted from Leslie Linthicum, "Men, Women, and Dirt," *The Albuquerque Journal, Sage Magazine,* July 1, 1990, p. 13.

Pages 52–53:
"It is a lot easier to feel sorry for ourselves . . ." Connell Cowan and Melvyn Kinder, "Wise Women, Wonderful Marriages," *McCall's*, April 1987, p. 180.

Page 55:
"Love does not consist in gazing . . ." The memorable words of Antoine de Saint-Exupéry were discovered in Anthony Brandt's article, "The Partnership," *Esquire*, June 1984.

CHAPTER THREE: THE COURAGE TO MAKE WAVES

Page 57:
Findings from the Roper Poll were described in an excellent article by John Tevlin, "Why Women Are Mad as Hell," *Glamour*, March 1992, p. 206. Women's increasing anger at men is verified by the Virginia Slims Opinion Poll, which surveyed three thousand women. The survey found that only 51 percent of the women felt that men are basically kind and thoughtful, a decrease from the 1970 survey, in which 67 percent thought this. Cited in *Newsweek*, April 30, 1990.

Page 59:
"In advertising, before we sit down . . ." Helayne Spivak's advice was found in her article, "The Art of Standing Out in a Crowd," *Working Woman*, June 1991, p. 66. The similar do-your-homework strategy proposed by Ellen Belzer was described in her article, "The Negotiator's Art: You *Can* Always Get What You Want," *Working Woman*, April 1990.

Page 60:
"Goode suggests that we look at the 'sociology of the dominant group' . . ." William J. Goode's theory that men's dominance as a group influences their attitudes toward their power over women was presented in "Why Men Resist," *Rethinking the Family: Some Feminist Questions.* Edited by Barrie Thorne and Marilyn Yalom (New York: Longman, Inc., 1982).

One of the most important books about male/female power is Warren Farrell, *The Myth of Male Power* (New York: Simon & Schuster, 1993). Farrell points out how much of male power is an illusion, and makes us take a very different look at the balance of power between men and women.

Page 62:
". . . I couldn't handle being second in her life." The experience reported to *Wall Street Journal* reporter Mary Bralove was found in an article by Zick Rubin, "Are Working Wives Hazardous to Their Husbands' Mental Health," *Psychology Today,* May 1983.

"No matter how they scream, plead, or reason . . ." Shere Hite, *Women and Love: A Cultural Revolution in Progress* (New York: Alfred A. Knopf, 1987). This is a very insightful look at women's lives.

Pages 63–64:
"In the end, success isn't so much a matter of . . ." Madeline Prober wrote on the importance of developing a strong sense of self in "The Dynamics of Drive," *Glamour*, April 1990, p. 227. The importance of this concept was also revealed in a series of seminars for women in transition conducted by *Lear's*. The seminars, called "The Philadelphia Experiment," were described by Carol Saline in *Lear's,* March 1990, p. 96.

Page 64:
"Without a clear sense of 'I' we become . . ." Harriet Goldhor Lerner's insightful analysis was found in her book, *Dance of Intimacy: A Woman's Guide to Courageous Acts of Change in Key Relationships* (New York: Harper & Row, 1989).

Pages 64–65:

"Mothers sacrifice. Wives sacrifice." For an in-depth discussion of women, men, and sacrifice, see Claudia Bepko and Jo-Ann Krestan, *Too Good for Her Own Good* (New York: Harper & Row, 1990), and the article by Conalee Levine-Shneidman and Karen Levin, "Love Strategies," *Working Woman,* April 1985, p. 162.

Page 66:

The "selfhood scale" provided by Harriet Goldhor Lerner, *Dance of Intimacy, op. cit.*

An example of how a single behavior change can set off a chain reaction and become a start toward assertiveness was described by Jean Baer, *How to Be an Assertive, Not Aggressive, Woman* (New York: Signet, 1976), p. 19. One of my favorite books.

Page 67:

"We either make ourselves miserable or . . ." Carlos Castaneda, *Journey to Ixtlan* (New York: Simon & Schuster, 1972).

Page 68:

"In the depths of our minds we never . . ." A. G. Thompson's explanation of the sources of aggressive reactions against our partners was presented by Maggie Scarf in *Intimate Partners: Patterns in Love and Marriage* (New York: Random House, 1987), p. 184.

Page 70:

"When we are facing the bad behavior of someone . . ." Further information on controlling anger in the workplace can be found in Kathryn Stechert Black's article, "Can Getting Mad Get the Job Done?" *Working Woman,* March 1990, p. 86.

Page 74:

"Autonomy simply isn't a value that society . . ." Dr. Anne Jardim's comments from her book *The Managerial Woman* (Garden City, New York: Anchor Press, 1977) were quoted by Madeline Prober, "The Dynamics of Drive," *Glamour,* April 1990, p. 227.

Page 75:

The profile of Hillary Clinton was found in Patricia O'Brien's excellent article, "The First Lady with a Career?" *Working Woman,* August 1992. Also see Vivian Cadden's article, "Hillary Clinton: Working Mom in the White House?" *Working Mother,* September 1992.

Page 77:

The factors associated with career success for women were identified by a study conducted by the Center for Creative Leadership, headquartered in Greensboro, North Carolina. The research results were described in an article entitled "Women with Promise: Who Succeeds, Who Fails?" *Working Woman,* June 1987. It was authored by Ann M. Morrison, Randall P. White, Ellen Van Velsor, and the Center for Creative Leadership.

Page 80:

"The person with whom I share a marriage . . ." W. W. Meade's story was found in his article, "Changing Men, Changing Marriage," *Working Woman,* November 1986, p. 170.

Page 81:
"There are times when only anger will make the necessary point . . ." Carol Tavris, *Anger: The Misunderstood Emotion* (New York: Simon & Schuster, 1982), p. 253.

"We are being strengthened by it . . ." Marcia Appel's comments on anger were quoted by John Tevlin, "Why Women Are Mad as Hell," *Glamour*, March 1992.

CHAPTER FOUR: THE GENTLE ART OF NEGOTIATION

Page 83:
"Yet others quietly, . . . Janet Horton, "The Art of Negotiation," *New Woman*, July, 1991, p.74.

Page 86:
"The goal of . . ." Francis Roe, MD, personal communication.

"Winning negotiators . . ." Gerald Nierenberg quoted in Morton Hunt, "How to Come Out Ahead," *Parade*, September 4, 1988.

Pages 87–88:
"Collaboration takes time . . ."Pat Heim and Susan k. Golant, *Hardball for Women: Winning at the Game of Business.* (Los Angeles: Lowell House, 1992) p.57. This is a terrific book, one that should be given to girls when they graduate from high-school and be required reading for every woman.

Page 89:
"Remember . . ." Psychologist Barbara Brown excellent advice is from a series of personal interviews conducted for this book.

Page 90:
Jimmy Calano and Jeff Salman's experience with lawyers appeared in "Tough Deals, Tender Tactics" an article they wrote for *Working Women*, July, 1988.

Page 91:
"You can't negotiate . . ." from Michael Korda's insightful article, "Partnership," *Self,* February, 1982. He makes this point better than anyone else.

"approach your colleague . . ." Robert Bramson quoted in Diane Cole's "Handling Difficult Co-Workers," *Working Mother,* April, 1992.

Page 94:
Pate Glacel's advice quoted in Cole, *Ibid.*

Page 97:
"Try to figure out . . ."Mary Beth Sullivan quoted in Horton, *op.cit.*

Page 103:
J. M. Gottman's study quoted in Ollie Pocs, *Our Intimate Relationships: Marriage and the Family* (New York: Harper & Row, 1989), p. 207.

Deborah Tannen, author of *You Just Don't Understand: Women and Men in Conversation,* is quoted in an article by Leslie Linthicum, *Sage Magazine,* July 5, 1992, p. 12.

Page 105:
"Because men and women are able . . ." Leslie Linthicum, *ibid.*

Page 106:
Judith Sills quoted in Kim France, "Sleeping with the Enemy," *Mademoiselle,* October 1991, p. 147.

Howard Markman quoted in Karen S. Peterson, "Husbands Want to Fight by the Rules," *USA Today,* October 27, 1989, p. B-1.

Page 107:
Mark Sherman and Adelaide Hass's research appeared in "Man to Man, Woman to Woman," *Psychology Today,* June 1984.

Jane Cambell, "Male Answer Syndrome," *Utne Reader,* January/February 1992.

Page 109:
Alfie Kohn, "Girl Talk, Guy Talk," *Psychology Today,* February 1988.

Also see Lillian Glass, *He Says, She Says: Closing the Communication Gap Between the Genders* (New York: Putnam, 1992).

Page 111:
Pat Heim and Susan K. Golant, *op. cit.*

Pages 111–112:
Sally McConnell-Ginet quoted in Kohn, *op. cit.*

CHAPTER FIVE: DEALING WITH THE REALITY OF UNEQUAL PAYCHECKS

Page 113:
"Most people like to think . . ." Philip Blumstein and Pepper Schwartz, *American Couples: Money, Work, Sex* (New York: Wm. Morrow & Co., 1983), p. 53.

Pages 114–115:
According to the article, "Wage Gap Between Men and Women Widens," by Patricia Lamiell (AP), in *The Albuquerque Journal* 12–17–92, "Women earned 70 cents for every dollar earned by men in 1991, down from 72 cents in 1990. While women's wages jumped to 75 percent of men's during the first three quarters of 1992, that was because men's wages dropped faster than women's did—not because women's wages went up."

Also, Grace Weinstein, "Making the Most of Two Paychecks," *Working Mother,* April 1992 states: "In fact, according to statistics women's earnings have hovered at around 60% of men's for more than 30 years . . .

"Though 70% of the improvement for women in the earnings ratio from 1979 to 1987 was from increases in women's earnings, the other 30% occurred because men's wages fell in manufacturing."

Page 115:
". . . 82 percent of the women replying . . ." Shere Hite, *Women and Love: A Cultural Revolution in Progress* (New York: Alfred A. Knopf, 1987).

"While the wives might be more likely to manage . . ." Financial planner Michael Stein's comments were quoted by Vivian Marino, "More Women are Working but Men Still Rule Family Financial Roost," *Albuquerque Journal,* May 21, 1990.

Page 119:
"When couples do take the time . . ." Philip Blumstein and Pepper Schwartz, *op. cit.,* pp. 53, 89.

Page 123:
"It's important for a woman trying to deal with . . ." Harriet Braiker, "Who Is the Right Man?" *Working Woman,* January 1987. Dr. Braiker is a contributing editor of *Working Woman.*

"When it comes to managing my finances . . ." Natalie Angier, "Fear of Finance," *Mademoiselle,* January 1989.

Page 124:
"Women are still in a very transitional role . . ." Marilyn Cohen's observations were quoted by Vivian Marino, *op. cit.*

Page 125:
"I suffer from a chronic case of financial phobia . . ." Angier, *op. cit.,* p. 114.

"When I was working as an investment broker . . ." Anne Kohn Blau's remarks quoted in Grace Weinstein, "Making the Most of Two Paychecks," *Working Mother,* April 1992.

Page 126:
"We live with so many money myths . . ." Psychologist Olivia Mellan's insightful analysis of the meaning of money was found in Angier, *op. cit.,* p. 115.

Page 127:
Comments by Michael Stein and Victoria Felton-Collins concerning women's failure to take an active role in family money management were quoted by Vivian Marino, *op. cit.*

Also, Claudia Taylor, an account executive for Boettcher and Company in Albuquerque, New Mexico, notes that "a recent poll in a business magazine revealed that 85 percent of working women don't know the nature of their companies' pension plans." Claudia Taylor, "Take Charge of Your Life by Taking Charge of Your Money," *Women,* Fall 1990.

Page 128:
"Often, it's not until death or divorce . . ." Jan Warners, lawyer and financial counselor, was quoted by Weinstein, *op. cit.*

Pages 128–129:
"Almost three-fourths of elderly Americans . . ." Results of a study by the Older Women's League (OWL) and a hearing held by the House Subcommittee on Retirement Income and Employment reported in Don McLeod, "Retirement Far From a Golden Pond for Women in Pension Crunch," *AARP Bulletin*, July/August 1990, vol. 31, no. 7.

Page 129:
"You don't have to be versed in macro-economics . . ." Financial planner Connie S. P. Chen, in Angier, *op. cit.*, p. 151.

CHAPTER SIX: WHEN SHE EARNS MORE THAN HE

Pages 132–133:
"Being equally successful . . ." in Julia Kagan, "Who Succeeds, Who Doesn't," *Working Woman*, October 1985.

Page 133:
Wives' earnings from D. Abramson, "The sex/love/money/power game," *Glamour*, May 1988.

Page 135:
"To be a man . . ." Demos quoted in Jessie Bernard, "The Good-Provider Role: Its Rise and Fall," *American Psychologist*, vol. 36, no. 1, January 1981, pp. 1–12. Roger Gould quoted in same article.

Pages 136–137:
Experiences of couples where the husband moved when his spouse got a better job quoted in Gary Libman, "Men put their wives' career ahead of own," *Fort Myers News Press*, August 25, 1988.

Page 138:
Lisa Silberstein quoted in Julie Connelly, "How Dual-Income Couples Cope," *Fortune*, September 24, 1990, p. 134.
"From childhood . . ." Pete Hamill, "Great Expectations," *Ms.*, September 1986.

Page 139:
Philip Blumstein and Pepper Schwartz, *American Couples: Money, Work, Sex.* (New York: William Morrow & Co., 1983).

Page 143:
"The trick is . . ." Sonya Rhodes, "The Nice Way to Tell Your Husband What Bugs You," *McCall's*, June 1992, p. 74.

Page 145:
"You can't solve . . ." Nancy Arann quoted in Maggie Mahar, "Trading Places," *Working Woman*, July 1992, p. 161

Page 146:
"I would have thought . . ." Ann Fisher quoted in Robin Givhan, "Equal Pay for Women Still Far From Reality," *Albuquerque Tribune,* July 12, 1990.

Page 147:
"It's embarrassing . . ." Baila Zeitz quoted in Linda Lehrer, "More than She Bargained For," *Ms.,* January/February 1989, p. 113.

Page 148:
"When women succeed . . ." *American Couples, op. cit.*

Page 149:
"Many working women . . ." Ruth Rosenbaum quoted in Maggie Mahar, *op. cit.,* p. 61.

Page 150:
Judith Sills quoted in Maggie Mahar, *op. cit.*
"When we picture . . ." Warren Farrell, *Why Men Are the Way They Are* (New York: McGraw-Hill, 1986), p. 171.
"Because of the way . . ." Rosenbaum quoted in Maggie Mahar, *op. cit.*

Page 151:
"It's tough . . ." Joe's story from Gary Libman, *op. cit.*

Page 154:
"Women traditionally see . . ." Anthony Astrachan, *Why Men Feel: Their Response to Women's Demands for Equity and Power* (New York: Anchor Press, 1986), pp. 212–213.

Page 156:
Julie Connelly, "How Dual-Income Couples Cope," *Fortune,* September 24, 1990. Rod Hills is quoted here.

Page 157:
"Women come from . . ." Carole Wade quoted in Linda Lehrer, *op. cit.*

Page 158:
"Men are reluctant . . ." Linda Lehrer, *op. cit.*

CHAPTER SEVEN: MEN AND THE GREAT DUST BALL CAPER

Page 159:
"We used to be . . ." Patricia Mainardi, "The Politics of Housework," written over twenty years ago. It continues to be quoted because it is still relevant. It reappeared in *Ms.* in May 1992 as an "Instant Classic."

Page 161:
The Second Shift: Working Parents and the Revolution at Home (New York: Viking, 1989) is a landmark book by Arlie Hochschild. She found that working women do 75 percent

of the housework and that only 18 percent of the husbands share housework equally. And the more the husbands earned, the less they did at home.

Joan Huber and Glenna Spitze's research was mentioned in an interview with Arlie Hochschild and cited by Cynthia Gorney, "Fry It Up in a Pan Yourself, Buster," for *Special Report,* August/October, 1990, p. 39.

"The happiest two-job marriages . . ." *Ibid.*

For another insight into the household chore imbalance see Susan Faludi's review of Mary Kay Blakely's book, *Wake Me When It's Over* (New York: Times Books) in *Ms.,* June 1989. In this article she also takes a close look at the problems Hochschild discussed in her book, *op. cit.*

Page 162:
"Whether you're meeting with clients . . ." Helanye Spivak, "The Art of Standing Out in a Crowd," *Working Woman,* June 1991, p. 66.

Page 165:
Jesse Barnard's theory of "his" and "her" marriage can be found in her classic book, *The Future of Marriage* (New York: Bantam, 1972).

Page 167:
List of men's attitudes from several sources including Linda Thompson and Alexis Walker's review of the literature in "Gender in Families: Women and Men in Marriage, Work, and Parenthood," *The Journal of Marriage and the Family,* vol. 51, November 1989.

Page 168:
How men created family "myths" that let them live with values and practices is from Hochschild's *The Second Shift, op. cit.*

Page 169:
The report of household tasks appeared in Debra Kent's article, "Sex and Housework," *Working Mother,* September 1992.

For studies on men and housework see Linda Thompson and Alexis Walker's review of the literature in "Gender in Families: Women and Men in Marriage, Work, and Parenthood," *Journal of Marriage and the Family,* vol. 51, November 1989. Also of interest is the study entitled "Birth Timing and the Division of Labor in Dual-Earner Families," by Scott Coltrane, University of California, Riverside. Coltrane found that postponing the transition to parenthood facilitated task-sharing by encouraging men to become attached to the father role and encouraging women to relinquish some of their responsibility for household management. Coltrane's work on this subject was published in *Journal of Family Issues,* vol. 11, no. 2, June 1990, pp. 157–181.

On the issue of power and men's ability to get out of housework, see Thompson and Walker's *op. cit.* and Juanita Firestone and Beth Anne Shelton's "An Estimation of the Effects of Women's Work on Available Leisure Time," *Journal of Family Issues,* vol. 9, no. 4, December 1988, pp. 478–495. Also see Yoshinori Kamo, "Determinants of Household Division of Labor," *Journal of Family Issues,* vol. 9, no. 2, June 1988: pp. 177–200 and Maureen Perry-Jenkins and Ann C. Crouter, "Men's Provider-Role

Attitudes: Implications for Household Work and Marital Satisfaction," *Journal of Family Issues,* vol. 11, no. 2, June 1990, pp. 136–156.

Page 170:
"Many men . . ." Sonya Rhodes, "Housework: How to Make Your Husband Do His Fair Share," *McCall's,* November 1992. Another good article is Annie Gottlieb, "How to get people to do what you want," *McCall's,* March 1992.

Also, for a great laugh read Judith Viorst's, "Honk if you've heard these excuses," *Redbook,* January 1991, pp. 20–21.

Page 171:
"It should be . . ." is from Ken Druck's terrific advice in "Why Am I the One Who Is Always Responsible for Our Marriage?" by Ken Druck and Kathleen Duey, *Q,* February 1987.

"You can say, 'I have the feeling you think housework . . .'" Sonya Rhodes, *op. cit.*

"There are men . . ." from Druck's article, *op. cit.*

Page 172:
Druck's suggestions from his article, *op. cit.*

Page 173:
"Make sure your request . . ." Bruce Younger, and "People usually relate better to concrete . . ." Muriel Prince Warren, quoted in Morton Hunt, "How to Come Out Ahead," *Parade,* September 4, 1988.

Page 174:
Patricia Mainardi, "A man can cook . . ." quoted in Linda Thompson and Alexis Walker, "Gender in Families: Women and Men in Marriage, Work, and Parenthood," *Journal of Marriage and the Family,* November 1989, pp. 845–871.

Page 175:
"How can you expect . . ." from Susan Moller Okin, "Change the Family, Change the World," in *Utne Reader,* March/April 1990.

Page 177:
I found Mary Lynne Heldmann's comments from an article she wrote for *Working Woman,* date unavailable.

Page 179:
"Making room for opinions . . ." Nancy Austin's articles on managing for *Working Woman* are always excellent and witty to boot. She has the uncanny ability to get to the core of the situation. This article "Why Listening's Not As Easy As It Sounds," appeared in the March 1991 issue.

"Good criticizing . . ." Sonia Rhodes, *op. cit.*

Page 184:
Helayne Spivak's great example of how to get someone's attention is from "The Art of Standing Out in a Crowd," *Working Woman,* June 1991, p.66.

AFTERWORD: THE JOURNEY: FROM WOMAN TO WOMEN

Special thanks for the inspiration about how the bluebirds got to be in charge to Harriet Miller, director of the Women's Bureau of Fort Wayne, Indiana.

How to get involved in political action:

1. If you can't locate a local chapter call National Women's Political Caucus at (202) 898-1100. NWPC has three hundred chapters around the country.

2. Check your local directory for a chapter of NOW, usually listed under *Organizations* in the Yellow Pages.

3. If you can't locate the League of Women Voters' telephone number in your area, call headquarters in Washington, D.C.: (202) 429-1965.

FINANCIAL MANAGEMENT RESOURCES

Publications

AARP information pamphlets. AARP makes information available to women pertaining to pensions, Social Security, and personal savings. Two such pamphlets, available free of charge, are: "Protect Yourself—A Woman's Guide to Pension Rights" (D12258) and "Guide to Understanding Your Pension Plan" (D13533) Both free pamphlets can be obtained by addressing a postcard to the publication's title and number in care of AARP Fulfillment (EE057), 1909 K Street N.W., Washington, D.C. 20049.

The Consumer's Guide to Disability Insurance. This is a must-have publication that details how to survive a financial setback resulting from an illness or disability. For information, write to Health Insurance Association of America, P.O. Box 41455, Washington, D.C. 20018.

Financial Planning Especially for Women. This booklet, by Grace W. Weinstein, provides comprehensive information about the fundamentals of financial planning. To obtain a copy, write to Community and Consumer Relations, American Council of Life Insurance, Health Insurance Association of America, 1001 Pennsylvania Avenue N.W., Washington, D.C. 20004-2505.

The Social Security Book: What Every Woman Absolutely Needs to Know (American Association of Retired Persons, Rev. Sept. 1991). A comprehensive guide to Social Security benefits and how to obtain them. For information about this publication, write to AARP, 601 E Street N.W., Washington, D.C. 20049.

Unbalanced Accounts: Why Women Are Still Afraid of Money, by Annette Lieberman and Vicki Linder (New York: Atlantic Monthly Press, 1992). A good book to kick-start better management of your money.

Workshops

Women's Financial Information Program (WFIP). These community-based "fiscal fitness" workshops are organized under the auspices of the American Association of Retired Persons (AARP), and are now available in forty-eight states. Information about upcoming seminars may be obtained by contacting Barbara Hughes, AARP, WFIP, 601 E Street N.W., Washington, D.C. 20049.

INDEX